Walk Without Feet
Fly Without Wings
and
Think Without Mind

GW00750965

FULL
CIRCLE

FULL CIRCLE

Walk Without Feet
Fly Without Wings
and
Think Without Mind

OSHO

responding to disciples' questions

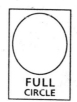

FULL
CIRCLE

WALK WITHOUT FEET, FLY WITHOUT WINGS AND
THINK WITHOUT MIND

Published by FULL CIRCLE
18-19, Dilshad Garden
G.T. Road, Delhi-110095
Tel: 2297792, 93, 94 Fax: 2282332

Osho ® is a registered trademark of
Osho International Foundation, used under license.

Compiling & Editing by Ma Yoga Anurag
Coordination by Swami Amano Manish

This Edition, 1999
ISBN 81-7621-046-3

Printed at Nice Printing Press, Delhi-110051
PRINTED IN INDIA

Contents

Bhagwan Shree Rajneesh
is now known simply
as Osho.

Osho has explained that
His name is derived
from William James' word
'oceanic' which means
dissolving into the ocean.
Oceanic describes the
experience, He says,
but what about
the experiencer? For that
we use the word 'Osho'.
Later He came to find out
that 'Osho' has also been used
historically in the Far East
meaning
"The blessed One, on whom
the Sky Showers Flowers."

Introduction

I hear your voice
and the sky is falling in
OSHO
oh
OSHO.

Listening to you speak
on these early mornings is to dissolve
between the walls
of a dewdrop.
Hearing your voice
my fight goes limp and oh comes the
love flood.
OSHO
since I have been here with you
my insides glow
a shrine in some liquid
gold.

Ten mornings
Tenderly showering

Ten thousand
delights.

At 7:30
dewdrops are full.
At 8:00
like hundreds of wet buds,
silent disciples are waiting for the sun
and he enters
to a symphony of breath.

The very first time I saw Osho
I could've sworn he wore roller skates... yes
he seemed only a freshly ironed white robe,
a shining robe
skating smoothly to that green chair
from which he speaks.

Friends,
This is a man who walks without feet!
And rumour has it that on each new moon
just at the split second that the cycle shifts
and the moon disappears
he can be seen hanging upside down
between the stars....

This man flys without wings.
He may very well breeze through your chest,
tickle your heart
this very moment! Oh lucky you
if he becomes your guest.
Oh lucky you!

Here in these pages
lies his response to the questions
that for ten days were seeds for his discourses.

An unusual happening:
at the last minute
Osho put aside the writings of Shankaracharya
that had been scheduled for discussion for these days,
and questions from folk like you and me
became the sutras for each of these ten mornings.
Lucky you, you are about to taste the nectar
of these mornings.
This is no ordinary book —
its secret lies behind your breath as you read.
It's not the philosophy, no —
not the wealth of information here,
not even the useful tidbits that brighten your day.
This is something else...

Osho speaks about parents and their children, about trusting
and creativity and surrender; he speaks on sex and responsibility
and jealousy, love, enlightenment, pornography; on play and
desirelessness and belief in God...

And it's something else.
Reading this book can be a meeting with the Master.
And that
is the sweetness here, not just in the words, or the
answers he gives.

"The meeting is the solution; not the answer, not the question
— the meeting. The point where my consciousness touches
your consciousness... Watch my answers! They are not really
answers to your questions, they are just like hammers. I try
to destroy your questions — sometimes politely and sometimes
not so politely. But the whole effort is to destroy the
questions."

This book will take you
gently,
deeply,
inside yourself to where you've never journeyed.
Here is a rare opportunity to let armours melt and
barriers drop,
to encounter a man
living in God.
He has arrived home.

Osho is a presence,
a hot emerald,
a scrumptious silly guy on roller skates.
He is something utterly internal.
And reading his words
ten thousand birds
may fly and sing
in your heart.

Ma Prem Maitri

CHAPTER
1

Fly Without Wings

The first question :

Osho, what exactly, in simple words, are you trying to teach? What is your exact message to humanity at large? — Again in simple language that I can understand.

WALK WITHOUT FEET
FLY WITHOUT WINGS and
THINK WITHOUT MIND

*T*HAT'S MY TEACHING. It cannot be made more exact than that. Life is so mysterious that you cannot reduce it to exact formulas. That is not possible. That will be unjust and unfair to life. A mystery has to remain a mystery.

If you reduce the mystery to a formula, you are being violent to reality. No explanation can explain away life. No fact can contain its truth.

You ask me : WHAT EXACTLY, IN SIMPLE WORDS, ARE YOU TRYING TO TEACH?

Only some negative things can be said — that I am trying to destroy the mind; that I have come to destroy, not to fulfill... because unless the old mind is destroyed utterly, the new will not be born. It is out of destruction that creativity arises. It is out of death that life blooms.

My whole work here consists in destroying the mind, its hold upon you; in destroying the roots of the mind so that you can be free in each moment of your life, so that you can be without a past. To be with a past is to be in a prison. The bigger the past, the more you are burdened with it. The more you are burdened with the past, the more you become incapable of living in the present. Then the present is only a word — you don't experience it. And truth is always in the present. Past is only memory, and future imagination. One is no more; one has yet to be. Between the two is this small precious moment.

And you can be in contact with this precious moment only if there is no mind. Mind means past and future. Either the mind thinks of that which has gone, or of that which is to come; either of yesterdays or of tomorrows.

Jesus says to his disciples : Look at the lilies in the field — how beautiful they are! Even Solomon in all his glory was not arrayed as one of these. And they spin not, they weave not, they work not. They don't think of the morrow... What is the beauty of the lilies in the field? They live in the present.

Except for man, the existence knows no past, no future. Except for man, there is NO misery. Except for man, there is no hell.

By destroying your mind and your past, I am bringing you back home so Adam can enter again into the Garden of Eden.

But don't ask me to be exact — that I cannot do. I cannot do it because I respect life so much. And I cannot be untrue to life. How can I be exact about a roseflower? And how can I be exact about the innocent eyes of a child? And how can I be exact about the beautiful form of a woman? How can I be exact about the clouds in the sky, and the rivers and the mountains and the stars? Life is so elusive, so mysterious, and life is such flux... everything continuously changing.

If you become too exact, you start losing contact with life. You have to be AS inexact as life is. You have to be as volatile as life is. You have to be continuously on the move! Life is not a noun — it is a verb. You have to be as much of a verb as life is... it is a process.

About dead things you can be exact, because they are no longer growing. All their potential is exhausted; there is no more to them. Definition is possible. You can be exact about a corpse, but you cannot be exact about a child. He may be here this moment and the next moment he may be outside in the courtyard. You cannot be exact! But if a corpse is lying there in the room, you can be exact that it will be lying there in the morning too.

Life is dynamic. Life is a dynamism. And I teach LIFE itself, so I cannot be exact.

That's where I differ — I differ from theologians, theoreticians, philosophers. They ARE exact. Their VERY exactness destroys their beauty and their truth. If they are so exact, they can only be wrong, they cannot be true. How can you define something which is growing? Here you define... and the thing has moved beyond your definition. While you are defining, the thing has been moving beyond your definition. How can you demark something which is expanding? There is no way.

And if you demark, then you will start looking at your demarcation and you will start forgetting life — because life will be very disturbing to you. That's why philosophers don't look at life; they are never existential. Even the philosophers who call themselves existentialists, even they are not existential. They are speculative. They weave theories in their minds. And they force life to conform to their theories. Life becomes crippled and paralyzed.

That's what Hindus and Mohammedans and Christians have done to truth — they have ALL paralyzed it. And they feel very sorry : "Why has truth died in the world?" They are the murderers! Who has killed God? Not the atheists, certainly. How can they kill? — they don't even believe. How can they kill? — they cannot find Him. To kill the God, you will need to find Him first. Who has killed the God? —these theoreticians, these people who are very exact, these clever and cunning and calculating people, these mathematicians, these systematizers. Their theory is more valuable than life itself. They become obsessed with the theory.

I have no theories. I am like a mirror. If it is morning, I say it is morning. If it is no more morning, I don't say it is morning — then it is no more morning! Each moment I reflect whatsoever is the case. I live in suchness.

And you ask me : WHAT EXACTLY, IN SIMPLE WORDS, ARE YOU TRYING TO TEACH?

Why do you ask this question? You would like to cling to some theory. You cannot get hold of me — that is your trouble. You want to catch hold of me.

One day, a professor came to see me and he said, "Why don't you write a small book in which all that you want to say is contained? — like the Christian catechism."

That is ugly. To me, that is ridiculous. He wants me to say how many gods there are — one, two or three? When God created the world — four thousand years before Jesus? On what day, in how many days He created the world. Whether He rested on Sunday or not? How many souls there are in the world? Whether there is rebirth or not. What the virtues are and what the sins are? He wants me to be very definite and clear.

It is not possible — because the thing that is virtue in the morning may become sin in the evening. And the thing that was sin in the morning may become virtue in the afternoon — one never knows. Something is true in one context and becomes untrue in another context. Something is beautiful one moment, and the next moment it turns ugly, sour, bitter.

LIFE IS NOT A THING! Things can be defined. Matter can be defined. That's why science is exact and religion can never be exact. The day religion is exact, it is dead. Don't ask me to be exact. How can one be exact? You can be exact about water, that it evaporates at a hundred degrees heat — you cannot be exact about man.

Man is unpredictable. The higher you go, the more unpredictable you become. A Buddha is absolutely unpredictable. You cannot catch hold of him; you cannot have him in your fist. He is like the vast sky. And there are so many nuances and so many colours and so many songs! And there is such variety! How can one be exact? And there is so much contradiction and there is so much paradox — how can one be exact?

No, I cannot be disrespectful to life — just to provide you with an exact answer? so that you can cling to it, so that you can become knowledgeable? so that you can go back home and say to your people that this is the teaching, this I have learnt?

The question is asked by Dr. B. P. Arya, from Nairobi. He must be in a hurry to catch hold of what my teaching is and go to Nairobi and tell people that "This is his teaching!" No, I will not allow you that knowledgeability. I DESTROY KNOWLEDGE! I don't help you to become knowledgeable — I help you to become more ignorant, more innocent, because life happens when you are innocent. When you don't know, you are available : when you know, you are closed.

So this is my teaching :

WALK WITHOUT FEET
FLY WITHOUT WINGS and
THINK WITHOUT MIND.

Mind means knowledgeability. Who is asking this question about exact teaching? — the mind. The mind cannot tackle the elusive, the mysterious. The mind can only tackle the arithmetic, the logical. The mind is incapable of understanding a song. The mind can only understand a syllogism. It is the mind that is asking... and I am the enemy of the mind.

And you ask : IN SIMPLE WORDS...

NO WORD CAN CONTAIN IT. There exists NO word that can contain life. There exists NO word that can contain love! There exists no word that can contain God!

Sufis have ninety-nine names for God. One wonders : Why not a hundred? Ninety-nine? One more they could have created. But there is a great message in it. They say : The real name is left blank, the hundredth, because God cannot be contained in any word. Ninety-nine are just toys to play with — because you ask, because you CANNOT be at ease with a nameless God, because you feel uncomfortable. You want some name for God so that you can address Him. If God is nameless, you feel impotent — what to do then? How to address...? where to look for...? what name to repeat?

So ninety-nine names are given, but even those ninety-nine names do not indicate anything. They indicate the hundredth, and the hundredth is just no word, emptiness. These ninety-nine names are nothing but ninety-nine names of nothingness, and the hundredth is nothingness itself. Those are toys for children to play with. But they are dangerous toys, because children have forgotten the hundredth completely and they have become engrossed in the ninety-nine.

Once a Sufi was staying with me and he used to repeat God's names, chanting morning, evening, in the night.... And I would ask him again and again: "When will you remember God?" And he was a little worried why I asked —he was remembering continuously, morning, evening, night. Two, three days and I was asking again and again, "When will you remember God?"

He said, "What do you mean? I go on remembering Him. Can't you see my lips moving continuously? Can't you see my rosary? I am moving the beads!"

I said, "These are ninety-nine names, but when will you remember God? When will you throw these beads? When will you stop your movement of the lips? When will you stop your inner chattering, inner talk, this constant repetition of those ninety-nine names? They have to go —only then does silence descend. And silence is mysterious. And silence cannot be contained in any sound. Truth cannot be forced into a word; the word is so small."

And you ask me IN SIMPLE WORDS — simple or difficult, it makes no difference. ALL WORDS ARE EQUALLY INADEQUATE. There are not a few words which are less inadequate and a few which are more adequate —all are absolutely inadequate. If you want to know what truth is, you will have to listen to my silence, you will have to listen to my being.

And you ask : WHAT EXACTLY, IN SIMPLE WORDS, ARE YOU TRYING TO TEACH?

I am not trying — I am simply teaching! Why should I try? But I know from where the question comes : you are always trying. People are trying to love, trying to pray, trying to meditate, and BECAUSE they are trying, they never love. How can you love when you are trying to love? If you are trying to pray, you CANNOT pray, because your energy will be moving in your trying. When you are trying to meditate, who will meditate? You are involved in the trying.

A Zen Master dropped his handkerchief on the floor, and a disciple was there and the Master said, "Try to pick it up and give it back to me. Try!"

And the disciple immediately took the handkerchief from the ground and gave it to the Master, but the Master dropped it again and he said, "I am saying *try* to get it!"

Six times the Master goes on dropping, and the disciple is puzzled as to what he *means*. Then suddenly the idea struck him : "The Master is saying *try* to get it." He said, "But how can I try? Either I pick it up or I don't. How can I try?"

And the Master said, "That's what you have been doing for three years — trying to meditate. Either you meditate or you don't! How can you try?"

Trying is a device. Trying is a trick. When you don't want to do a thing, you try. When you want to do a thing, you simply DO it!

Your house is on fire — do you try to get out? You simply get out! You don't try — you don't consult maps, you don't look into the scriptures. You don't think, "From where and how should I get out? Whom to ask? Where to find a Master who knows how to get out?" You don't think whether it is right to jump from the window, whether the book of etiquette allows it or not. Should one go from the front door or from the back door? You may even escape from the toilet! It doesn't matter — when the house is on fire, these things are immaterial, irrelevant. And you don't try... you simply get out! In fact, you don't even think; you will think when you are out. Then you will stand under a tree and you will take a good breath and you will say, "Thank God that I managed to get out!" But in fact you were not even thinking when you were getting out of the house. It was SO immediate.

When you come across a snake on the path, what do you do? Do you try to think how to jump, from where, how to escape? You simply jump! That action is total and that action is not of the mind.

That's what I mean :

THINK WITHOUT MIND
WALK WITHOUT FEET
FLY WITHOUT WINGS

Move into the immediacy of life.

I am not trying to teach : I AM my teaching. The way I am, the way I look at you, the way I talk to you, the way I say something or I don't say something — all that is part. It is not that I am separate from my teaching and trying to teach you. I am my teaching. And if you want to learn, you will have to be in tune with me.

Don't ask such foolish questions.

And you ask : WHAT IS YOUR EXACT MESSAGE TO HUMANITY AT LARGE?

WHERE IS HUMANITY? Have you ever come across humanity? You always come across human beings, never humanity. Humanity is an abstraction, just an empty word. The concrete and the real is the human being, not humanity. Don't be befooled by such great words.

People ARE befooled. I know a man : he was a colleague; while I was teaching in a university he was also a professor there. He is incapable of love, but he loves humanity. He is INCAPABLE of love, but he cannot accept that incapacity. It hurts. He cannot love any human being because his expectations are too great. He asks perfection. Now, you cannot find a perfect human being. This is a trick to protect yourself from love. This is a way to avoid : ask the impossible — it will never be fulfilled and you will never come to know your impotence.

He cannot love a woman, he cannot love a man — he cannot love. He is simply cold. And naturally so : he is a professor of logic — very cold. His heart has stopped beating; only his head is becoming bigger and bigger and bigger. He is becoming top-heavy. Any day he will topple. And he will say always that he loves humanity.

I asked him, "How do you manage to love humanity? Just give me a few instances. I would like you to be in love with humanity, but where do you find humanity? I would like to see you holding hands with humanity, embracing humanity, kissing humanity — I would like to see it."

He said, "What are you talking about? — humanity is not a person."

Then what is humanity? Has anybody ever seen humanity? 'Humanity at large' means nothing; it is just an abstraction. It is the idea of Plato. It is like you have seen one horse, another horse, another horse, and then you start thinking of the idea of 'horseness'. Have you ever come across a person who loves horseness? That will look foolish. Either you love horses or you don't — but horseness? What is that thing?

It is the same with 'humanity'. You come across this woman, this man, this saint, this sinner, but you never come across humanity. Humanity is just an idea created by the philosophers. But you can become obsessed with the idea and that can function like a protection. It protects that man from falling in love with an ordinary human being. And still he can go on thinking that he is a great lover — he loves humanity at large.

I am not concerned with humanity at all. I am not concerned with abstractions. I love human beings. And I have no expectations from them. I simply love them as they are. I don't ask for perfection. I don't ask that they should fulfill any conditions. As they are they are beautiful.

The moment you ask anybody to fulfill a condition, you are destroying, you are violent. You are not respecting the person. You are degrading him, you are insulting, humiliating him. If you say, "Be such and then I will love you," then you don't know what love is. Love is unconditional.

My love is for human beings, and my message too is for

human beings. I have nothing to do with abstractions like humanity. I deal with the concrete, with the real.

You ask : WHAT IS YOUR EXACT MESSAGE TO HUMANITY AT LARGE?

No message for humanity, but for human beings :

WALK WITHOUT FEET
FLY WITHOUT WINGS and
THINK WITHOUT MIND

For human beings, for you, for him, for her — but not for humanity. Not for Hinduism, not for Mohammedanism, not for Christianity, but for concrete human beings.

My message is : Drop the mind and you will become available to God. Become innocent and you will be bridged with God. Drop this ego, drop this idea that you are somebody special, and suddenly you will become somebody special. Be ordinary and you will become extraordinary. Be true to your inner being and all religions are fulfilled.

And when you don't have a mind, then you have a heart. When you don't have a mind, only then does your heart start pulsating, then you have love. No mind means love. Love is my message.

The second question :

You have said all enlightened ones, all religions, agree on one thing only. Their disagreements are many, but there is one agreement amongst all and that is that man, because of his ego, is closed to reality — the ego is the only barrier.

Why is it that all enlightened ones agree on only one thing when they can experience reality as it is? Would not they agree on many things since they don't have the clouds or barriers of the ego present to colour their perceptions?

WHEN THERE ARE NO MORE ANY CLOUDS, when your perception is clear, you see the sky — but the sky is indefinable, indescribable, AWACHYA, unspeakable. Nothing can be said about it, and whatsoever you say will be wrong. But the enlightened ones HAVE to say something about it, because you go on asking and you are not capable of listening to silence — so they have to say something!

Buddha says one thing, Christ says another thing; they are invented things. They cannot agree about those things. That is Buddha's choice : when he faces you he has to say something to you, to convey something to you, knowing perfectly well that whatsoever he is saying is going to be misunderstood. But there is no other way to have communication with you! Even if he wants you to come closer to him, to understand his silence, even if he wants to share his joy with you, he will have to use words to call you closer and closer.

Now, it is HIS choice to use certain words. Christ chooses different words; that is his choice. Patanjali chooses still others, Lao Tzu still others. They don't agree about those words, they can't agree. There is no need — they are all arbitrary. They agree about only one thing : drop the ego, drop the mind. About that they all agree.

Then what happens? — they have different stories to tell. Those stories are all invented stories; they have nothing to do with reality. They are just compromises with you, just to hold your hand a little longer so you can become infected with the Buddha. Just to hold your hand a little longer, a Buddha has to talk to you.

If he is allowed his own way, he will never talk. Exactly that happened : when Buddha became enlightened, for seven days he remained silent. There was no point in talking! That which had exploded in his being was so vast, there was no way to relate it to others. There was not a single word to indicate towards it. His silence was absolute. The story is beautiful :

Gods in heaven became very much disturbed, because it rarely happens that a man becomes a Buddha, and if Buddha kept quiet then the message would be lost. And a few beings were there who could be helped by the Buddha. And the gods came to Buddha and prayed to him : "You speak, sir!"

Buddha said, "But what is the point? First, whatsoever I say will not be true."

The gods said, "We know it will not be true, but it will attract a few people, and then slowly, slowly, you can lead them towards truth. Let them come! If you don't speak, nobody will ever come — then how will you lead them to silence? Let words be just traps, JUST traps, to catch hold of people. Let words be just seductions, because people only understand words. Once they are caught in the net of words, then you can take them anywhere you want —but first let them be caught!"

Buddha again said, "But they will not understand — they will MISUNDERSTAND. They have ALWAYS done that — misunderstanding — they will do that again. What is the point?"

The gods said, "But there are a few people, very few, certainly, who can be counted on the fingers — they will understand."

Buddha insisted again; he said, "Those few who will be able to understand me will be able to reach on their own. I don't think that they really need me. Maybe on their own they will take a little longer, but those who can understand me are aware enough — they will reach the truth on their own. I need not bother about them. And those who will NOT understand me, why should I bother about them?"

The gods were in much difficulty as to how to convince Buddha. Then they conferred amongst themselves : "What to do? This man seems to be stubborn!" They discussed, argued among themselves, and they brought a legal point. They said to Buddha, "You are right : there are many who will not understand you, who will CERTAINLY misunderstand you; for them, your speaking is not needed. And there are a few who WILL understand you, but they are very few, and you are right : they will reach the truth even without you. But between these two, do you think there is nobody? Between these two there are a few who will not go to truth if they don't get caught by you. AND they will not MISunderstand you. They may not be able to understand you immediately, but they will not misunderstand you! There is a category between these two categories : think of those."

And Buddha could not find anything against it. It looked so logical — and Buddha was a man of logic. He spoke for those few. But whatsoever he says, there are two things in it : one, the negative part of it. The negative part is : drop the ego, drop the concept of self. About that ALL enlightened people are in agreement. Once the ego is dropped, then what happens? Then they are not in agreement — not that truth is separate, but truth is vast.

Just think : three blind men are told by a physician, "This medicine will help you, this will cure your eyes. One thing is certain," says the physician, "that your eyes have to be cured, that your blindness has to be dropped." Now, all these three blind men are cured and they are standing here in the garden, and they go home and they all three relate what they have seen — do you think they will agree about it? they will say the same things? About one thing they will agree, that their blindness has disappeared. But what happened after the blindness disappeared will be totally different. Somebody may have seen the colours of the trees, the rainbow, the sun. Somebody else may not have been interested in the trees and the rainbow and the sun; may have looked at people, the faces, eyes, children laughing, joking; and somebody else may have seen something else.

Those three blind people will agree on one thing, that blindness has to be dropped. But what happens after blindness is dropped will be different — although the world they open their eyes on is the same; but it is a vast world, multi-dimensional. They will choose according to themselves. And their choice will depend on their likings, dislikings, aptitudes, types.

For example, Buddha says : When the ego is dropped THERE IS NO MISERY. Just look at his words : no misery. He never uses the word 'bliss'; whenever he says it, he says 'no misery'. Now this seems to be a little roundabout. Why should he say 'no misery'?

Mahavir says 'bliss'; when the ego is dropped, you are utterly blissful. And Buddha says : Misery disappears; you are in a state of no misery. There is a great difference, their choice is different, their framework is different. Mahavir always likes positive words. Buddha always likes negative words.

And Buddha says : With positive words there is a difficulty, and the difficulty is that they create greed — so he will never use them. For example, if you talk about blissfulness then people become greedy, desire arises. Everybody starts thinking, "I should become blissful! I should have this bliss this Buddha is talking about — I MUST have it." And the problem is : if you become desirous of bliss, you will not have bliss. The very desire will be the obstruction.

So Buddha says : By talking positively you have destroyed the possibility. The man has become more greedy! First he was greedy about the house and the money and the power and the prestige, now he is greedy about God and bliss and SATCHITANAND and truth — but he is still greedy. Now his desire is even bigger. He is entangled more in desire. You have not helped him — you have even harmed him. So Buddha says : I am not going to use any positive words. All positive words create desire in people's minds. I will say only that there is no misery.

It has some point, some valuable point in it. You don't become greedy about no misery. Just think of the words 'no misery', 'there will be no misery' — you don't feel any greed, you don't feel very enthusiastic about that state of no misery. It does not create desire. And Buddha says : Only WITHOUT desire can that state be attained.

But Mahavir also has a point. He says : If you talk about no-misery, no-self, people will not feel enthusiasm. Now what Buddha thinks will not create desire, Mahavir thinks people will feel no enthusiasm for. Who feels enthusiasm for no-misery? Why should one meditate for years and years just to attain a state of no-misery? That does not look very appealing. Why should one go into SADHANA — into work upon oneself — just to attain a state of no-selfhood? You will not be there. Just to attain no-selfhood, who will bother? People will become unenthusiastic; they will lose nerve, they will not be attracted towards religion. So Mahavir says : I have to use positive words — 'bliss', 'freedom', 'absolute selfhood'.

Both are right and both are wrong. With words, that is the problem. No word is absolutely right and no word is absolutely wrong — it depends on how you look at those words.

That's why they don't agree in anything else. Just about one thing they agree : that the ego has to be dropped.

The third question :

On day, as you talked about the new commune, I felt as though someone was hitting me again and again in my stomach until I thought I would vomit. Was that you? If it was, what are you up to?

HAVE YOU EVER HEARD that St. John of the Cross used to vomit during his ecstasies? Vomit can be of infinite significance. It can be a kind of unburdening. It can be not only indicative that the body wants to unburden — it can be indicative of the deeper psyche too, because the body and the soul are not separate, they are one.

Whatsoever happens in the body happens in the soul too; whatsoever happens in the soul happens in the body too — they vibrate together.

It happens many times that when your inner being wants to release some garbage, your body will also release some garbage. And when your body releases some garbage, you will feel as if your mind has also become clean. Have you not felt that kind of cleanliness after a good vomit? Have you not felt a quality of calmness after a good vomit? It not only relieves your stomach, it not only relieves your physical system of some poison — corresponding to it, something in your psyche is also released.

You say, Shaila : AS YOU TALKED ABOUT THE NEW COMMUNE...

The day I was talking about the new commune, many of you felt many things.... When I was talking about the new commune, it is natural that you started thinking about yourself — whether you will be acceptable in the new commune? whether you are worthy enough for the new commune? That is natural; for that idea to arise is natural — because the new commune will be the birth of a new man.

We will be creating an alternative world, a small alternative world. We will be moving in different dimensions than the people outside. We will be dropping all taboos, inhibitions, repressions. We will be vomiting all that the society has forced on you, that the society has stuffed you with. That's why the hammering was felt in the stomach.

All the languages of the world have such expressions : when you cannot accept something you say, "I cannot stomach it." When you have to accept something against yourself, you say, "I had to swallow it somehow." The stomach is not just physical — it is as much psychological as it is physical; it is psychosomatic. That's why whenever your emotions are disturbed, your stomach is immediately disturbed.

A man who is constantly angry cannot have a good stomach. A man who is aggressive cannot have a good stomach. A man who is worried will have ulcers, cannot have a good stomach. The stomach is the place where you are joined together : the soma and the psyche, both are joined there in the stomach, in the navel. The navel is the meeting point of matter and soul.

That's why in Japan to commit suicide people hit just under the navel. The navel is called HARA — that's why in Japanese suicide is called HARAKIRI.

Have you not watched it, observed it, that fear is felt just exactly two inches below the navel? If you are driving and suddenly you see some accident is going to happen and it is beyond control, where are you hit? Where do you feel hit? Deep in the stomach below the navel.

Listening to me, Shaila, on that day, you must have felt this hammering in the stomach, because to become real sannyasins you will have to vomit much. You will have to vomit all your education and all your religion and all your culture and all your civilization. To become a real sannyasin you will have to become primally innocent — you will have to become children again.

And that is going to be the work in the Commune : to efface all that the society has burdened you with, to make you a clean slate; to make you again wild, to make you again as innocent as children are, as innocent as animals; to make you again as innocent as the trees and the rocks. Certainly, much will have to be vomited; your stomach will have to be cleaned physically and spiritually.

Yes, it was I who was hitting — excuse me...!

The fourth question :

How can I see you,
How can I recognize you, Osho?

An ancient saying :

When the sun rises
we know this,
not by staring at it,
but because we can see everything ELSE clearly.

HOW DO YOU RECOGNIZE THE SUN? You don't stare at the sun — you look at the trees, you look at the people... you look all around : everything is so clear. Because everything is so clear, you know the sun has risen.

The only way to see me is if I can help you to see clearly around yourself. That's what I am doing here : making things clear, giving you a clarity, sorting things out, putting things in their right places, giving you vision and insight.

The day you can see things clearly — your desires, your

greed, your anger, your rages, your violence, your misery — the day you can see that it is you who are creating all this hell, the day you can see that you have NEVER been out of paradise, that you were just under a nightmare, the deeper you recognize it, the deeper you see it, the deeper your clarity, the more you will see me, the more you will recognize me. There is no other way!

I cannot give you any proof. What proof can the sun give to you that "I have come"? Should it bring some certificates from some court? Should it quote scriptures : "Look! In every scripture it is written that I will be coming"? No, that is not the point.

That's what people were asking Jesus. "How should we recognize you? How can we believe that you are the Messiah? Prove it!" And the Christians have been doing that for two thousand years, trying to prove from the Old Testament and other scriptures that : "Yes, the old Prophets declared, and this is the man about whom they declared that he would be coming."

This is foolish. This is absurd. Jesus cannot be proved by any declaration by anybody else. Who are these prophets to declare? And who are these old scriptures? And why should they control? Jesus stands in his own right — and those who want to see him should see him by the clarity that he brings. There is no other way.

If I bring some clarity to you, then you have seen me and you have recognized me. Don't look for any other proofs. There are none, and I am not interested in them at all.

But that seems easier, to have a proof : so that you need not think, so that you need not bother, so that you can accept something because of the old, ancient authorities. No, I stand here on my own feet. I am not standing on anybody's shoulders. I will not take the help of Buddha. Buddha has declared, "I will be coming after twenty-five centuries," and the time has come. People write letters to me : "Are you the Buddha?" No. I stand on my own feet. I would not like to burden Buddha and stand on his shoulders — mm? — that will be so unmannerly. I can stand on my own feet.

When the sun rises
we know this
not by staring at it
but because we can see everything else clearly.

Another ancient saying says :

There are none so blind
as those who do not wish to see.

Remember it : if you DON'T wish to see, then there is no way. If you wish to see, then you cannot avoid me. Just search for the wish, just search in your inner desire. If you have the passion to see me, then nothing can hinder you — you will be able to see me.

But if you DON'T want to see me, if you have some investment in NOT seeing me, not recognizing me, then there is a problem.

Somebody has written that "I am a Christian and I cannot believe that you are the Messiah." Now this is an investment. That's what the investment was with the Jews : they could not recognize Jesus because they were Jews. Now, you are a Christian and you cannot recognize me.... Hindus could not recognize Buddha because he had gone out of the tradition. Buddhists cannot recognize Kabir because he is not a Buddhist.

Just a few days ago, a man came to me from far away. And he said, "I have come to you to become a sannyasin because I am a follower of Kabir, and you have spoken such beautiful words about Kabir — that's why I have come."

He was not interested in me at all. I could see that he was not seeing me at all. Just to be respectful to him, I gave him sannyas. And I asked him, "Will you be staying here?" He said, "No, there is no need." "Would you like to do some meditations?" He said, "I am doing — I am following Kabir."

Now, this man, even though he thinks he has taken sannyas from me, has not even come to me. He is befooling himself. He has only come to me because I have spoken so beautifully on Kabir.

There are many who have come to me because I have spoken so beautifully on Christ, or so beautifully on Gurdjieff, or so beautifully on somebody else — but they have not come to me. They are not my people. Even if they are here they will not be able to see me — they have their investments.

The last question :

Beloved Osho, you wonderful, beautiful, marvellous trickster! Here we are —Bodhi, Vidya and Arup— walking home in the middle of the night, in drunken stupor of punch, beer, French wine and champagne, after two years of total abstention, just repeating in true Buddhist fashion "Stumbling, stumbling, drunk, drunk" ready to tumble into bed and alcoholic oblivion — and there is the note that suddenly tomorrow is question and answer day!

And two hours of typing, cutting and being aware, are ahead and, lo and behold! Where is the drunkenness? Gurdjieff is nothing compared to this. Roars of laughter and clarity in the head. Spelling mistake, spelling mistake.

Thank you for the device.

This is from Arup....

ARUP IF YOU HAD INVITED ME TOO, then I would not have troubled you at all. I had to change suddenly. I was going to start a series of talks on Shankaracharya's Atma-Bodha — self-knowledge. Looking into the sutras, it looked like an anti-climax to Buddha. The heights that we were flying with Buddha... and then the very ordinary and traditional sayings of Shankaracharya I felt it would not be good. It would be like falling from the peaks into the valleys. It would be like one had suddenly cut your wings.

Buddha was talking of no-self; and Shankaracharya will talk of self. Buddha was talking of no knowledge and Shankaracharya will talk of knowledge, self-knowledge. And Shankaracharya's statements are very, very traditional Hindu.

I could have managed, but it would have been too much effort. Hence, I thought it was better to say goodbye to Shankaracharya — and I have said goodbye to him forever!

CHAPTER
2

First Taste Your Own Being

Do you believe in you?
Do you believe in God?
Who is God?

*N*O, I DON'T BELIEVE IN ME... I CANNOT, BECAUSE I AM NOT. There is nobody to be believed in, and nobody to believe in it either.

If you believe in yourself, you believe in an illusion. The very belief will prevent you from knowing the reality.

Once you start believing in an illusion, you start losing contact with the real. To know the real, all illusions have to be dropped — and the greatest illusion of all is the ego, the 'I'.

You ask me : DO YOU BELIEVE IN YOU?
No, not at all. That's why I am able to know.
You ask : DO YOU BELIEVE IN GOD?

No again — because to believe in God is not to know Him. Belief is always out of ignorance. Those who don't know, they believe. If you know, what is the point of believing in? When you know, you know!

You don't believe in the morning sun. You don't believe in the trees and in the mountains. You NEED not! You know the sun is there. You know the people are there, you know the trees are there. There is NO question of belief. Why do you believe in God? Because you don't know.

You substitute your knowledge by belief. You hide your ignorance behind the belief. The belief gives you a pretension of knowing. All beliefs are pretentious. All beliefs are deceptions. Whom are you deceiving? You yourself are deceived.

When a man says, "I believe in God," he is saying he has not been able to know God — that's all he is saying. He is not strong enough to say it that way. He is not strong enough to see his own ignorance and accept it. Hence, he says, "I believe in God!" What is the need of believing in God if you know?

Knowledge never becomes belief. Knowledge remains knowledge. Ignorance tries to become belief. Remember always : whenever you believe, it is just to hide your ignorance. It is a cheap knowledge that belief gives.

I don't believe in God — because any relationship of belief is a wrong relationship. I know God... but to know God the only requirement is that I should not be. The moment you disappear, God appears. Only when you are spacious enough to contain Him, when you are no more there occupying inner space — in fact, absence of yourself is the presence of God.

Remember : you will never meet God. You cannot, because the meeting will mean you are also real and God is also real — then there will be two realities, not one. And reality IS one. If you are, God cannot be. If God is, you cannot be.

And the third thing you ask : WHO IS GOD?

God is not a 'who', He is not a person. God is the totality, the sum total of the whole existence. God is not somebody : God is 'allness'.

I am God, you are God — everybody is God, all is God. In fact, to use the word 'God' is not right. There is godliness and no God at all. To be really true to reality, 'godliness' is the right word to use, not 'God'. The moment you say 'God', many things arise out of that word....

First : God becomes a person — and God is not a person God is impersonal existence; God is impersonal 'beingness'. Once you say 'God', God becomes a 'he' —that is male chauvinistic, that is ugly. God is neither a 'he' nor a 'she'. And if you decide to use 'he' or 'she', then 'she' is far better — because 'she' includes 'he', but the 'he' does not include 'she': 'She' is far bigger — naturally so. Man is born out of the woman. The woman can contain the man, the man cannot contain the woman. The man has no womb to contain anything.

But both are wrong. God is neither man nor woman, because He is not a person at all.

Then what is God? Don't ask 'who is God?' ask 'what is God?'

Life is God. Love is God. Light is God. It is an existential experience. You never come across God like an object. You come across godliness — like an inner upsurge. Something blooms in you... and you cannot even find the flower, just a fragrance. God is not a flower but a fragrance.

I cannot indicate where God is, who God is. I can simply relate my experience of fragrance to you.

Existence is full of godliness. Everything is divine — the flowers, the birds, the rocks, the rivers.... Not that you have to create a temple for God and a church for God — that is stupid, because God is everywhere! For whom are you creating the temple and the church and the mosque? If you want to pray, you can pray anywhere. Wherever you bow down you bow down to God, because none else exists.

You will have to understand MY language. 'Belief' is a dirty word here. And by belief you are prevented from knowing; you are not helped. And it is because of belief that man is divided. It has not helped man's spiritual growth; it has been one of the greatest barriers. It is belief that divides you as a Christian, a Hindu, a Mohammedan. It is belief that divides the earth. It is belief that creates wars.

The MOMENT you believe, you are no more one with humanity : you are a Christian or a Hindu or a Mohammedan. You have gone ugly, you are poisoned! And now you will be continuously fighting for your belief. And all these people fighting for their beliefs are blind people fighting for their belief in light — and nobody knows what light is.

I have heard :

The policeman was walking his beat when he saw two men fighting and a little boy standing alongside them crying, "Daddy, Daddy!"

The officer pulled the two men apart and, turning to the boy, asked, "Which one is your father, lad?"

"I don't know," the boy said, rubbing the tears from his eyes, "That's what they're fighting about."

Do you really know who God is? You don't know even who you are — how can you know who God is? You have not even become acquainted with the closest reality — that is beating in your heart, that is breathing in you, that is alive in you — and you are thinking to become acquainted with the totality of existence? the infinite, the vast, the eternal? And you have not even been able to have a taste of your OWN being. You have not even tasted a single drop of the sea, and you want to taste the whole sea?

And you NEVER go to the sea! You go to the scriptures. You never go to the sea — you go to the priests. And then you create belief, and the belief comes out of your fear, not out of your love, not out of your knowing, not out of your experience — it simply comes out of your fear. You believe because alone you feel afraid; because you are childish, you want somebody to hang on to, to cling to. You need a father-figure! so that you can always look up to him, so that you can always throw the responsibility, so that you can always cry and weep and remain helpless.

It is out of your fear that you have created God. And a God created out of fear is ill, it is pathological. It will not bring you well-being : it will make you more and more pathological.

The so-called religious man is almost pathological; he is neurotic. Go to the monasteries, look around with open eyes, and you will be simply surprised that in the name of religion a thousand and one kinds of pathologies are practised. People don't become healthy and whole — they become more and more helpless, more and more frightened, more and more eccentric. Of course, their neurosis is such that it is respected.

Freud is right when he says that religion is a collective neurosis. I agree with him. The so-called religious ARE neurotic. If a single person behaves in that way, you will think he is mad; but if a big crowd behaves in that same way, you think it is religious.

Just the other night I was talking about a follower of Mahatma Gandhi; his name was Professor Bhansali. He took a vow of silence. Now, the real silence never arises out of vows. The very phenomenon of the vow indicates that the silence is imposed, false, pseudo, violent; otherwise, there is NO need to take a vow. If you have understood the beauty of silence, you will be simply silent! Why take a vow? Why decide for tomorrow? Why say that "From now onwards I will remain silent and I will not speak a single word"? Against whom are you taking the vow?

If you have known the beauty of silence, if you have experienced the joy of it, if you have melted in it, if you have flowed into it — what is the point? You never take a vow that "I will love my whole life — I take the vow." You don't take the vow that "I will eat my whole life." You don't take the vow that "I will go on breathing till I die." This will look foolish! You enjoy love — there is no need to take the vow. People take vows for celibacy, not for love — why? Because celibacy is unnatural, imposed. When celibacy is also natural, spontaneous, no vow is taken.

Now this man, Professor Bhansali — I knew the man — took a vow of silence, went to the Himalayas. For two years, three years, he remained in silence. It was a hard struggle; it was a continuous fight with himself — it was repression, great repression. He must have become split : the one who is trying to impose the vow and the one, the natural one, who wants to have a little chit-chat with people, or to talk, or to relate, communicate.

One night he was sleeping and somebody in the darkness walked over him. He was fast asleep. In sleep you cannot remember your vow. He shouted, "Who are you? Are you blind or something? Can't you see I am sleeping here?" Then he remembered that he had broken his vow. Naturally, he felt very guilty; great guilt arose in him. He had taken the vow and he had broken it! And he was really a masochist — otherwise, why should one take the vow of being silent?

Talking, communicating to people is such a joy! Why should one become enclosed into one's being? This is morbid. But now he was guilty — to punish himself he started eating cow-dung! But that was not enough. To punish himself, he sewed up his lips with a copper wire. Even that was not enough — insanity knows no limitations. He jumped into a cactus bush and rolled naked, thousands of thorns in his body, and he would not allow the thorns to be removed by anybody. There were wounds and wounds all over the body.

But he became very famous — he became a mahatma. People started coming towards him, worshipping him. Now, what will you call this man? Will you call him a mahatma? If you have any senses left in you, you will call him pathological. He needs psychiatric treatment, maybe electric shocks; he needs psychoanalysis. But he was a famous disciple of Mahatma Gandhi — just next to Mahatma Gandhi.

This has been happening down through the ages. There have been Christian saints who have been beating themselves every morning, wounding their bodies; and people would come to worship them and to see who was wounding himself more. And the person who was wounding himself more than others, of course, was a greater saint.

Now, these people who were wounding themselves, killing themselves slowly, they WERE pathological; and the people who used to come to see them, they were also pathological. The saints were masochists and the onlookers and the worshippers were sadists — they both were in a subtle ill state of affairs.

There have been saints who cut their genital organs. There have been women saints who cut their breasts. What will you call these people? But they live according to the belief — they are believers!

Man has to get rid of ALL this stupid kind of religiousness. Man has to get rid of all this nonsense that has persisted down the ages. It is because of this nonsense that religion has not become part of everybody's life.

No, religion need not be based on belief. Religion has to be based on experience — not on fear but on love; not on negation of life but on affirmation of life. Religion has not to be a belief — it has to be a knowing, an experiencing. That's why I say 'belief' is a dirty word here. 'Knowing', 'loving', 'being' — these are real words.

And, belief hinders them : you cannot know if you believe, you cannot love if you believe, you cannot see if you believe. And remember : I am not saying that you have to disbelieve, because disbelief is again belief. The atheist and the theist are not different — they are in the same boat, they are fellow-travellers. The theist believes God is, the atheist believes God is not — but BOTH believe. Their beliefs are antagonistic, but as far as belief is concerned both are believers. There is not much difference.

What I am saying is : neither belief nor disbelief is needed — because you don't know, so how can you believe? and you don't know, so how can you disbelieve? When belief and disbelief are both dropped, there is silence. When belief and disbelief have both disappeared, you are open to truth; then you don't have any prejudice, then your mind is no more projecting. Then you become receptive.

Neither believe nor disbelieve. Just be watchful, receptive, open! — and you will know.

And what you call that knowing does not matter — whether you call it God, or you call it enlightenment, or you call it nirvana, does not matter! These words are just words. Any word will do : X, Y, Z will do. But first you have to get rid of belief and disbelief.

Getting rid of belief and disbelief, you get rid of the mind. And only a state of no-mind comes to know. The state of no-mind is blissful....

The second question :

Is not Shankaracharya enlightened? — Then why did you drop the proposed series of talks on him?

HE IS ENLIGHTENED, PERFECTLY ENLIGHTENED. My dropping of the proposed series of talks does not mean that I am saying he is not enlightened. But his expression is run of the mill, very ordinary, mundane, traditional, conventional. His expression of his experience is ordinary.

Buddha's expression is extraordinary. Buddha's expression is special. That does not mean that their experiences are lower or higher — no. Enlightenment is enlightenment — there is no higher, no lower. What Buddha knows, Shankaracharya knows.

It is like this : you go to the Himalayas; you see the beauty of the Himalayas and the virgin silence, and those peaks covered for millions of years by pure snow — you feel it in every pore of your being; your every fibre vibrates with that benediction that the Himalayas is. You come. back and somebody asks, "Would you please paint a little picture so I can see something of your experience? I have not been fortunate enough to go to the Himalayas, but can't you paint a little picture?" Now there will be differences.

If a Van Gogh had gone to the Himalayas, he would have painted a totally different kind of picture; if you paint, it will not be a Van Gogh — you don't know how to paint. Still you have been to the Himalayas as much as Van Gogh has.

Or somebody says to you, "Can't you sing a song about your experience?" Now, songs will be different... they are bound to be different. A poet will be able to sing beautifully, will be able to compose poetry. Your poem will not be much of a poem; at the most a limerick — it cannot be great art. It will depend on your skill.

Buddha is a Van Gogh of that world, so is Tilopa, so is Saraha, so is Hakuin. These are aristocrats of that world! Shankara is ordinary. Even when I chose him, I had chosen very reluctantly. I was thinking to drop many sutras. There ARE a few diamonds, but ninety-nine percent is rubbish. If you search deep enough you will find a few diamonds, but ninety-nine percent is valueless.

Buddha's sayings are all diamonds — you will not find rubbish at all. In Shankara you may be able to miss the diamonds, but in Buddha it is impossible to miss, it is almost impossible to miss. You can miss one, you can miss two, you can miss three —how can you miss so many diamonds? a row of diamonds?

Shankara is enlightened as much as Buddha is, but his

expression is mediocre. That's why he has impressed the Indians very much! Buddha has not impressed; Buddha remained so high that he passed over their heads. Shankara has impressed them very much. Shankara is one of the most important names in Hinduism. Buddha has no place. What happened?

The mediocre mind found Shankara very appealing, close; there was some affinity between Shankara and the mediocre mind. And the crowd IS mediocre. To understand Buddha you will have to become an individual; to understand Shankara will be difficult if you are an individual — you will have to be of the crowd.

Shankara's statement is for the crowd. He went deep into the Indian mind; he impressed the Indian mind very much.

Buddha disappeared! The Indian mind lost track of Buddha; there was great distance. But if you want to go to the Himalayas, why not go to Everest?

That's why I dropped that series.

The third question :

Why are parents so cruel to their children? Is there any sense in making them responsible? And how can one avoid making the same mistake?

PARENTS ARE CRUEL TO THEIR CHILDREN because parents have some investment in them. Parents have some ambitions they would like to fulfill through their children — that's why they are cruel. They want to use the children. The moment you want to use somebody, you are bound to be cruel. In the VERY idea of using somebody as a means, cruelty has entered, violence has come in.

Never treat another person as a means! — because each person is an end unto himself.

Parents are cruel because they have ideas : they want their children to be this and that. They would like their children to be rich, famous, respected; they would like their children to fulfill their unfulfilled egos. Their children are going to be their journeys.

The father wanted to be rich but could not succeed, and now death is approaching; sooner or later he will be cut off from life. He feels frustrated : he has not yet arrived. He was still searching and seeking... and now comes death — this looks so unjust. He would like his son to carry on the work, because his son represents him. He is his blood, he is his projection, his part — he is his immortality. Who knows about the soul? Nobody is definite about it. People believe, but belief is out of fear, and deep down the doubt remains.

Each belief carries the doubt in itself. Without the doubt there cannot be any belief. To repress the doubt, we create the belief — but the doubt remains gnawing in the heart like a worm in the apple; it goes on eating inside you, it goes on rotting you from the inside. Who knows about God and who knows about soul? They may not be.

The only immortality known to man is through children — that is actual. The father knows, "I will be living in my son. I will be dead, soon I will be under the earth, but my son will be here. And my desires have remained unfulfilled." He imposes those desires, implants those desires, in the consciousness of his son : "You have to fulfill them. If you fulfill them, I will be happy. If you fulfill them, you have paid your debts to your father. If you don't fulfill them, you have betrayed me."

This is from where cruelty comes in. Now, the father starts moulding the child according to HIS desire. He forgets that the child has his own soul, that the child has his own individuality, that the child has his own inner growth to unfold. The father imposes HIS ideas. He starts destroying the child.

And he thinks he loves : he loves only his ambition. He loves the son also because he is going to become instrumental; he will be a means. This is what cruelty is.

You ask me : WHY ARE PARENTS SO CRUEL TO THEIR CHILDREN?

They cannot help it, because they have ideas, ambitions, desires — unfulfilled. They want to fulfill them, they want to go on living through their children. Naturally, they prune, they cut, they mould, they give a pattern to the children. And the children are destroyed.

That destruction is bound to happen — unless a new human being arises on the earth, who loves for love's sake; unless a new parenthood is conceived : you love the child just for the sheer joy of it, you love the child as a gift from God. You love the child because God has been so... such a blessing to you. You love the child because the child is life, a guest from the unknown who has nestled into your house, into your being, who has chosen you as the nest. You are grateful and you love the child.

If you really love the child, you will not give your ideas to the child. Love never gives any ideas, never any ideology. Love gives freedom. You will not mould. If your child wants to become a musician, you will not try to distract him. And you know perfectly well that being a musician is not the right kind of job to be in, that he will be poor, that he will never become very rich, that he will never become a Henry Ford. Or the child wants to be a poet and you know he will remain a beggar. You know it! but you accept it because you respect the child.

Love is always respectful. Love is reverence. You respect! because if this is God's desire to be fulfilled through the child, then let it be so. You don't interfere, you don't come in the way. You don't say, "This is not right. I know life more, I have lived life — you are just ignorant of life and its experiences. I know what money means. Poetry is not going to give you money. Become a politician, rather! or at least become an engineer or a doctor." And the child wants to become a woodcutter, or the child wants to become a cobbler, or the child simply wants to become a vagabond, and he wants to enjoy life... rest under trees, and on the sea beaches, and roam around the world.

You don't interfere if you love; you say, "Okay, with my blessings you go. You seek and search YOUR truth. You be whatsoever you want to be. I will not stand in your way. And

I will not disturb you by my experiences — because my experiences are MY experiences. You are not me. You may have come through me, but you are not me — you are not a copy of me. You are NOT to be a copy of me. You are not to imitate me. I have lived my life — you live your life. I will not burden you with my unlived experiences. I will not burden you with my unfulfilled desires. I will keep you light. And I will help you — whatsoever you want to be, be! with all my blessings and with all my help."

The children come through you, but they belong to God, they belong to totality. Don't possess them. Don't start thinking as if they belong to you. How can they belong to you?

Once this vision arises in you, then — then there will be no cruelty.

You ask : WHY ARE PARENTS SO CRUEL TO THEIR CHILDREN? IS THERE ANY SENSE IN MAKING THEM RESPONSIBLE?

No, I am not saying there is any sense in making parents responsible — because they have suffered because of THEIR parents, and so on and so forth.... Understanding is needed. Finding scapegoats is of no help. You cannot simply say, "I am destroyed because my parents have destroyed me — what can I do?" I know, parents ARE destructive, but if you become alert and aware you can get out of that pattern that they have created and woven around you.

You ALWAYS remain capable of getting out of any trap that has been put around you! Your freedom may have been encaged, but the freedom is such, is so intrinsic, that it cannot be utterly destroyed. It always remains, and you can find it again. Maybe it is difficult, arduous, hard, an uphill task, but it is not impossible.

There is no point in just throwing the responsibility, because that makes you irresponsible. That's what Freudian psychoanalysis has been doing to people — that is its harm. You go to the psychoanalyst and he makes you feel perfectly good, and he says, "What can you do? Your parents were such — your mother was such, your father was such, your upbringing was wrong. That's

why you are suffering from all these problems." You feel good —
now you are no more responsible.

Christianity has made you feel responsible for two thousand
years, has made you feel guilty, that you are the sinner. Now
psychoanalysis goes to the other extreme : it simply says you are
not the sinner, you are not to feel guilty — you are perfectly okay.
You forget about all guilt and you forget all about sin. Others
are responsible!

Christianity has done much harm by creating the idea of
guilt — now psychoanalysis is doing harm from the other
extreme, by creating the idea of irresponsibility.

You have to remember : the parents were doing something
because they were taught to do those things — their parents had
been teaching them. They were brought up by parents also; they
had not come from heaven directly. So what is the point of
throwing the responsibility backwards? It doesn't help; it will not
help to solve any problem. It will help only to unburden you from
guilt. That is good, the good part; the beneficial part of psychoanalysis
is that it unburdens you from guilt. And the harmful part is that
it leaves you there; it does not make you feel responsible.

To feel guilty is one thing : to feel responsible is another
thing. I teach you responsibility. What do I mean by responsibility?
You are not responsible to your parents, and you are not
responsible to any God, and you are not responsible to any
priest — you are responsible to your inner being. Responsibility
is freedom! Responsibility is the idea that "I have to take the reins
of my life in my own hands. Enough is enough! My parents have
been doing harm — whatsoever they could do they have done :
good and bad, both they have done. Now I have become a mature
person. I should take everything in my own hands and start living
the way it arises in me. I should devote all my energies to MY
life now." And immediately you will feel a great strength coming
to you.

Guilt makes you feel weak : responsibility makes you feel
strong. Responsibility gives you heart again, confidence, trust.

That is the meaning of sannyas. Sannyas wants you to be free from Christianity, Hinduism, Jainism, Mohammedanism, and sannyas wants you to be free from Freudian psychoanalysis and things like that too. Sannyas wants you to live your life authentically, according to your innermost voice, not according to any other voice from anywhere. Not according to the Bible or according to the Koran. If God has spoken in a certain way in the Koran, it was specifically meant for Mohammed, not for you. It was God's dialogue with Mohammed, not with you. You will have to find your own dialogue with God. You will have to find your own Koran!

If Jesus has spoken those beautiful words, they are out of the dialogue that happened between him and the totality. Now don't go on repeating them. They are meaningless for you. They are not BORN in you, they are not PART of you! They are like a plastic flower : you can bring a plastic rose and hang it on the rosebush — yes, they are like that — it is not the same as when a roseflower comes out of the rosebush itself.

You can deceive people. Those who don't know may be deceived. They may see so many beautiful flowers are blooming on the rosebush, and they are all plastic. But you cannot deceive the rosebush — you cannot deceive yourself. You can go on repeating Jesus, but those words have not been uttered in your ears by God; they are not addressed to you. You are reading a letter addressed to somebody else! It is illegal; you should not open that envelope. You should search and find your own relationship with the totality.

That relationship I call responsibility. Response means spontaneous capacity to relate. Response means capacity to respond to life situations according to your heart, not according to anybody else. When you start feeling that, you become an individual. Then you stand on your own feet.

And remember, if you stand on your own feet, then only one day will you be able to walk without feet and fly without wings. Otherwise not.

And you ask : AND HOW CAN ONE AVOID MAKING THE SAME MISTAKES?

Just try to understand those mistakes. If you see the point, why they are committed, you will not commit them. Seeing a truth is transforming. Truth liberates. Just see the point! — why your parents have destroyed you. Their wishes were good, but their awareness was not good; they were not aware people. They wanted you to be happy, certainly, they wished you all happiness. That's why they wanted you to become a rich man, a respected man; that's why they curbed your desires, cut your desires, moulded you, patterned you, structured you, gave you a character, repressed many things, enforced many things. They did whatsoever they could. Their wish was right : they wanted you to be happy, although they were not aware of what they were doing, although they themselves had never known what happiness is. They were unhappy people! and unaware.

Their wish was good — don't feel angry about them. They did whatsoever THEY could. Feel sorry for them, but never angry at them. Don't feel any rage! They were helpless! They were caught in a certain trap. They had not known what happiness is, but they had some ideas that a happy person is one who has much money. They worked for it their whole lives; they wasted their whole lives in earning money, but they remained with that stupid idea that money brings happiness. And they tried to poison your being too. They were not thinking to poison you — they were thinking they were pouring elixir in you. Their dreams were good, their wishes were good, but they were unhappy people and unaware people — that's why they have done harm to you.

Now be aware. Search for happiness. Find out how to be happy. Meditate, pray, love. Live passionately and intensely! If you have known happiness, you will not be cruel to anybody — you cannot be. If you have tasted anything of life, you will never be destructive to anybody. How can you be destructive to your own children? You cannot be destructive to ANYBODY at all.

If you have known awareness, then that's enough. You need not ask "And how can one avoid making the same mistakes?" If you are not happy and aware, you cannot avoid making the same mistakes — you will make the same mistakes! You are bound to, you are doomed to make the same mistakes.

So I cannot give you a clue as to how to avoid — I can only give you an insight. The insight is : your parents were unhappy — please, you be happy. Your parents were unaware — you be aware. And those two things — awareness and happiness — are not really two things but two aspects of the same coin.

Start by being aware and you will be happy! And a happy person is a non-violent person.

And always remember : children are not adult; you should not expect adult things from children. They are children! They have a totally different vision, a different perspective. You should not start forcing your adultish attitudes upon them. Allow them to remain children, because they will never be again; and once lost, everybody feels nostalgia for the childhood, everybody feels those days were days of paradise. Don't disturb them.

Sometimes it is difficult for you to accept the children's vision — because you have lost it yourself! A child is trying to climb a tree; what will you do? You immediately become afraid — he may fall, he may break his leg, or something may go wrong. And out of your fear you rush and you stop the child. If you had known what joy it is to climb a tree, you would have helped so that the child could learn how to climb trees! You would have taken him to a school where it is taught how to climb trees. You would not have stopped him. Your fear is good — it shows love, that the child may fall, but to stop the child from climbing the tree is to stop the child from growing.

There is something ESSENTIAL about climbing trees. If a child has NEVER been doing it, he will remain something poor, he will miss some richness — for his whole life. You have deprived him of something beautiful, and there is no other way to know about it! Later on it will become more difficult for him to climb on the tree, it will look stupid or foolish or ridiculous.

Let him climb the tree. And if you are afraid, help him, go and teach him. You also climb with him! Help him learn so he doesn't fall. And once in a while, falling from a tree is not so bad either. Rather than being deprived forever....

The child wants to go out in the rains and wants to run around the streets in the rain, and you are afraid he may catch a cold or get pneumonia or something — and your fear is right! So DO something so that he is more resistant to colds. Take him to the doctor; ask the doctor what vitamins should be given to him so that he can run in the rains and enjoy and dance and there is no fear that he will catch cold or will get pneumonia. But don't stop him. To dance in the streets when it is raining is such a joy! To miss it is to miss something very valuable.

If you know happiness and if you are aware, you will be able to feel for the child, how he feels.

A child is jumping and dancing and shouting and shrieking, and you are reading your newspaper, your stupid newspaper. And you know what is there — it is always the same. But you feel disturbed. There is nothing in your newspaper, but you feel disturbed. You stop the child : "Don't shout! Don't disturb Daddy! Daddy is doing something great — reading the newspaper." And you stop that running energy, that flow — you stop that glow, you stop life. You are being violent.

And I am not saying that the child has always to be allowed to disturb you. But out of a hundred times, ninety times you are unnecessarily disturbed. And if you don't disturb him those ninety times, the child will understand. When YOU understand the child, the child understands you — children are very very responsive. When the child sees that he is never prevented, then once you say, "I am doing something please..." the child will know that it is not from a parent who is constantly looking to shout at him. It is from a parent who allows everything.

Children have a different vision.

"Now, I want it quiet," said the teacher, "so quiet you can hear a pin drop."

A deep silence descended on the classroom. After about two minutes an anguished voice from the back shouted, "For Pete's sake, let it drop!"

It was the little boy's first day at school, and as soon as his mother had left him, he burst into tears. Despite all efforts on the part of his teacher and the headmistress, he went on crying and crying until finally, just before lunch, the teacher said in exasperation, "For heaven's sake, shut up child! It's lunchtime now, and then in a couple more hours you'll be going home and you'll see your mummy again."

At once the little boy stopped crying, "Will I?" he said. "I thought I had to stay here until I was sixteen!"

They have their vision, their understanding, their ways. Try to understand them. An understanding mind will always find a deep harmony arising between him and the child. It is the stupid, the unconscious, the non-understanding people, who go on remaining closed in their ideas and never look at the other's vision.... Children bring freshness into the world. Children are new editions of consciousness. Children are fresh entries of divinity into life. Be respectful, be understanding.

And if you are happy and alert, there is no need to be worried about how not to commit the same mistakes — you will not commit. But then you have to be totally different from your parents. Consciousness will bring that difference.

The fourth question :

I came to Pune because you are a Master and I have been seeking for one for a long time. How can I find out whether you are my Master? Will I only have to believe what you say about that or will I be able to recognize you? Somehow I am waiting for something to happen which will make my inner voice say "Yes" and surrender. My relationship with you just seems to be in my head, but I don't feel that I can do anything to change it. Can you?

FIRST, YOU SAY, I CAME TO PUNE BECAUSE YOU ARE A MASTER." Don't believe rumours. And you say, "I have been seeking for one for a long time." Why are you so against a Master?

Why are you seeking for so long a time? Why should you be so much interested in a Master? For what? You should seek yourself.

If you seek yourself, you will find the Master. The ancient saying is : When the disciple is ready, the Master appears. How can you seek a Master? You will not even be able to recognize one. You may come across... you may not be able to see.

Seek your own being! Go deeper into your own being, go deeper into your own silence. And then suddenly, when you need a Master, he will appear — he always appears.

Now, you are on a wrong track. And if you are looking too much for a Master, you will go on missing. At least while you are here for a few days, drop that search. Just be here and you may find. Meditate, dance, sing, and be here! Forget that search. Don't go on looking from the corner of your eye for the Master. Your very look, your very effort, your seeking, will prevent you. The very desire comes in between.

The relationship with a Master is possible only when there is no desire. In a non-desiring mind it happens.

And you ask : WILL I ONLY HAVE TO BELIEVE...?

No not at all. I am the last person to tell you to believe in me. Just be here with me, that's enough. If you ARE here with me, I am going to happen to you. It is a promise — but don't seek and search.

CHAPTER
3

Love Is A Resurrection

The first question :

What is herenow?
Does 'thought' form part of it?
If so, then all-time and all-things are now.
Or... Is herenow only in no-mind?

$\mathcal{D}$IVYA, THOUGHT IS THE CAPACITY OF NOT BEING HERE — so thought cannot exist in the herenow, it cannot be part of it. That is impossible. Thought can only be either of the past or of the future. Thought can never be of the present. In the VERY process of thinking, that is implied; it is intrinsic to it.

The moment you think, either you think of the past or you think of the future. It may be the immediate past, but it is still past — it is never the present, it cannot be the present.

Thought needs space. And the present moment has no space in it. Thought creates the past and the future to live in. The bigger the past, the more easily thought can move; the bigger the future, again, the more easily thought can move. The present is not capable of giving that space for thought to move.

The present moment is a moment of no-mind. Whenever you are in the present you don't function as a mind. Your body is in the present but your mind is never. Your body is ALWAYS in the present — that's why the body is so beautiful and mind is so ugly.

And, down the ages, you have been taught to be with the mind and against the body. That has been the greatest calamity humanity has suffered up to now. If a new humanity is to be, we will have to put things right — you have to be with the body and not with the mind.

Use the mind, but never get identified with it. The mind is a good slave, but a very bad master. The body is wiser.

When you are hungry, you are hungry herenow; you cannot be hungry in the future and you cannot be hungry in the past.

When you are feeling thirsty, your throat is feeling it right now —
it is immediate, it has a presence. But your mind is running in
all directions... so your body and mind never meet. That's how
you have become split, that's how schizophrenia has entered into
the very being of man.

Get out of the mind and get into the body. The more you
are in your body, the more natural you will be. The more you
are in the body, the closer to God you will be.

Mind is just a device. Good! Helpful! Can be used in a
thousand and one ways! But it is from there that the problem
arises — because it can be used in so many ways, you start
becoming dependent on it and by and by you lose consciousness
of the present and you become focussed with the mind. Then
your life will be dry, a wasteland.

And suddenly questions will arise : What is the meaning of
life? — because mind cannot supply any meaning. Mind cannot
give you any end. Mind cannot help you to live. It cannot give
you life! It can give you technology, it can give you bigger
machines, it can give you more affluence —but it cannot give you
more life, more being.

So riches go on growing. Technology goes on becoming more
and more sophisticated... and man becomes more and more poor.
This is strange! that outside riches go on accumulating and inside
man becomes a beggar. Never before in the history of man was
there such inner emptiness, such inner meaninglessness, such
inner poverty.

The reason is : significance comes from the body — the body
is the body of God. Mind is man-created : body is still in God,
it still exists in God, it still breathes God.

You ask : WHAT IS HERENOW?

Now, if any mind answer is given to you, that won't be the
right answer — because anything that the mind can say as a
definition of herenow will be wrong; anything whatsoever, it will
be wrong. Mind knows nothing of herenow! How can it define
it? Just be silent; for a moment, just be... and it is there.

THIS is herenow! I will not give you a definition, because definitions come from the mind, and definitions will be taken by the mind, and herenow is an existential experience... these trees, this bird calling, and the traffic noise, and the train, and the sun and the trees... and you, and me... and this silence, this presence....

When not even a single thought is stirring in you, when the screen is utterly empty, not even a single picture moves... this is... and this cannot be defined. You can experience it; it is available. It is everybody's RIGHT to experience it, but how to define it? If you try to define it you will have to bring past and future. Go to the dictionaries, go to the Encyclopedia Britannica — what will they say? They will say the present is a moment between the past and the future — that's the only way to define it! Now can there be a more wrong way to define the present? If you have to bring past and future into the definition, if you cannot define the present without bringing past and future into it, how are you going to define it?

The present is neither past nor future — AND IT IS NOT BETWEEN THE TWO! It CANNOT be between the two, because the past is no more and the future is not yet. How can the present be between two non-existentials? The present is existential; how can existence be defined by something which is not? That is utter absurdity! But that's where logic moves. Logic appears very logical, but remains rooted in absurdity.

The present is not between the past and the future : the present is beyond past and future. The present is eternity. The present is not even part of time! And it is not that the time passes : we pass, time remains; we come and go, time remains. It is not that the moment that was here just a moment before has become past, no. It is a single moment, utterly one. It is eternity. It is not passing, it is not going anywhere.

Have you not observed some time, sitting in a train, waiting on a station, and your train starts moving and you feel the other train has started moving which is just on the other track? Or, the other train starts moving and you feel your train has started moving, and then you look closely and you find that, no, your train is not moving, the other train is moving.

Time remains there — WE go on moving, WE change. The ocean of time is there — the fish goes on moving. The movement is in our minds. Mind is movement. Truth is unmoving; it is always the same.

Just see : when you were born... have you changed since then? Yes, on one level you have changed, certainly — your body has grown, you are young or old, and so many things you have lived through, and experiences, and frustrations, and excitements, and ecstasies, and all that life gives.... But go deep down : have you really changed on THAT plane? at the very core of your being? Are you not the same? There nothing has changed. It is where you were, and it is where you will ever be — it is always the same there, it is one climate.

On the surface things go on changing. The wheel of the cart goes on moving, but it moves on something which remains unmoving : the axle. You are both the circumference and the axle, the centre. Even the cyclone is not there at the centre — there is silence. Nothing ever moves there.

THAT IS YOUR BEING! What name you give to it matters not. That centre of the cyclone... that centre of the cyclone is herenow; it is not part of time. It is eternity.

You ask me : WHAT IS HERENOW?

Feel it! Experience it! That's what we are doing here! What IS meditation? — getting into here... now. What is love? — getting into herenow. What is celebration? — getting into herenow. But no definition is possible.

Getting-into IS possible, because in fact you have never got out of it. It is there! You can again turn and face it.

While making love to a woman or to a man, have you not felt the herenow? If you have not felt it then you have not loved. Making love to a woman, have you not forgotten the past? has not the past utterly disappeared in that moment? In that moment do you have a past, a history, an autobiography? If you have, then you don't know how to love. Then you have been just playing the game of love not knowing exactly what it is — you have not loved.

While making love, your autobiography simply disappears. There is no more any past — as if you had never existed. You are not OLD — in that moment you are virgin newness; in that moment you are born for the first time; in that moment there is rebirth. Love is resurrection. And there is NO future. Is there tomorrow? While making love to your woman, are you thinking of the tomorrow? what you are going to do tomorrow? Then you are not with the woman and you are not in love either. All thinking stops — that's the joy of love!

That's why I say that sex and samadhi are joined together. Sex is the lowest rung, samadhi is the highest rung, of the same ladder. They belong to the same ladder — sex the lowest rung, samadhi the highest rung. But the ladder is the same. There is an affinity.

Man got the idea of samadhi from two things : sex and sleep. Deep sleep is also on the same ladder. Man became alert to the phenomenon of samadhi, became excited, intrigued, by the phenomena of love and sleep — because in both these moments, time disappears, time stops, mind stops, thinking no longer functions — and because thinking no longer functions and time stops, there is such ecstasy and such joy. Then man became intrigued : Is it possible to attain this joy without falling into sleep? — because in sleep it happens, but you are not aware of it; it is very unconscious. Only in the morning do you hear the distant sound of it, or the later effects. If you slept deeply in the night, in the morning you feel renewed, rejuvenated — but you had not been there exactly while it was happening. What was it?

In sex, you are more aware, but then the sex moment is so small that rather than satisfying you it leaves you very much frustrated. The greater the experience of love, the greater will be the frustration that comes in its wake. Remember : only great lovers are frustrated with love; ordinary lovers are not frustrated with love — because the higher the peak, the greater will be the fall. And the peak exists only for a single moment. It comes and it is gone... it is like lightning.

And when the peak is gone, you have known the taste of it and now NOTHING will taste better and everything will look ordinary compared to it, and everything will look mundane. You have experienced something of the sacred. You have experienced something of God — God flashed like lightning, but you could not catch hold of His face, you could not figure it out, how He looks, and He was gone. It was so fast and so sudden.

Man became interested : Is it possible to prolong that experience? Is it possible to remain in that experience a little longer? Is it possible to go into it a little deeper? Is it possible to have that experience without moving into sex? — because sex by its very nature depends on the other. It is a kind of dependence, and all kinds of dependence destroy your freedom. That's the eternal fight between the lovers.

They are giving something to each other which is immensely valuable, but mixed with poison. They cannot live separately and they cannot live together. If they are separate they start missing the joy that was happening through the other; if they are together, the poison is too much — and one starts thinking : Is the joy worth it? Because you have to depend on the other! When you depend on the other, your freedom is destroyed, your freedom becomes defined, confined, limited. You cannot open yourself as you would like to open. You have always to look to the other and the other's feelings. You feel prevented, hindered. And the other starts possessing you, the other starts becoming powerful over you — because the other knows that it is through him or her that you feel joy.

Man started looking for the same experience without becoming dependent on the other. Then, if it depends only on sexual experience, it cannot last forever. You can have sex once in a while — and what about the other times? All other times you will remain dull and dead. Is it possible to have that joy continuously, as a continuum, like a river flowing always?

These were the speculations of man, but they came from sleep and love. In love sometimes it happens, and that is the moment which is called orgasm. If time stops, if thinking stops, and you are UTTERLY herenow, it is orgasmic.

This orgasmic experience will give you the taste. I cannot define it, but I can indicate ways how to feel it.

IF YOU HAVE SOME AESTHETIC SENSE, then some aesthetic experience will give you the taste. Seeing a sunset, if you have the heart of a painter, the heart stops; you start missing beats. The sun is setting, just falling and falling... and a moment more and it will be gone. And all that colour in the clouds, and all that sublime beauty! And the birds returning back to their homes, and the silence settling on the earth, and the trees getting ready to go to bed, and the whole of nature saying goodbye to the sun.... If you have the aesthetic heart, if you are a poet or a painter or a musician, if you know what beauty is, if you ARE affected by beauty, not so-so but tremendously, if beauty gives you awe — then you will know what herenow is.

Or listening to music it happens sometimes. There is nothing more meditational than music. Or if you can play some instrument yourself, then it is far better — because listening you remain on the periphery; playing you are at the centre. If playing some instrument — playing a flute or sitar or guitar — and you are LOST into it, absolutely lost into it, time stops, mind is no more there, a Buddha moment arrives, and you know what herenow is.

Or if you can dance — which seems to me the most profound experience — if you can dance and dance so deeply that the dancer disappears, only the dance remains, then again YOU will be herenow.

I cannot define it, but I can indicate a few things. You will have to experience it. It is a taste! If you ask me how sugar tastes, how can I define it? I can say it is sweet, but that will not make much sense — it will be a tautology. You were asking what sweet is; I have simply substituted another word for it If I say to be herenow means to be in the present, I am not saying anything — I am simply substituting another word for it. That's what dictionaries go on doing.

All dictionaries live on tautologies. And if you look into the dictionary you will be surprised : ask the philosopher or the philologist "What is mind?" and he says "Not matter"; and then ask him "What is matter?" and he says "Not mind" — but what is the point of it? You don't know either. When it comes to defining matter you use 'mind' as if you know mind, and you say "Not mind"; and when it comes to defining the mind you start using 'matter' as if you know matter, and you say "Not matter" — but you don't know either. Now, two things themselves undefined, how can they define each other? — that is not possible.

Ask the philologist who knows words and languages — what does he go on saying? You ask one word, he substitutes another word for it — but the real problem remains.

A Zen Master was dying and the disciples had gathered. And his whole life he had been talking about herenow — that's what Masters have been doing down through the ages. The disciples asked again, "Master, you are leaving us and we will be left in darkness. Is there any last message so that we can cherish it and remember it forever? We will keep it as a sacred memory in our hearts."

The Master opened his eyes... at that moment on the roof of his hut, a squirrel ran making noise — TIT TIT, TEEVEE, TIT TIT — and the Master raised his hand and said, "THIS IS IT!" and died.

What is he saying "This is it"? He is simply indicating. He is simply saying there is nothing to say — there is much to see, but there is nothing to say.

You ask : DOES THOUGHT FORM PART OF IT?

No, thought cannot form part of it. It is asking : Does darkness form part of light? Just like that. Darkness cannot form part of light. When light is present, darkness is absent; when light is absent, darkness is present — they never meet. So is the state of mind and herenow — they never meet.

Herenow means no-mind. No-mind means no thought. And you know it! Many times it happens to you : there are moments, small, but they ARE there, when you suddenly see no thought stirring in you, no ripple arising — those are Buddha moments! You just have to get more in tune with them, you just have to get deeper into them, you just have to change your emphasis.

For example, you read a book. Naturally, you read the words printed on the paper; you don't see the paper. The paper remains in the background. The words written with the black ink, they are the figure, and the white paper is the background. You may not even see the white paper while you are reading — although it is there! Without it, those words cannot exist; they exist because of it, against it, in contrast to it.

It happened : a psychologist did a small experiment. He fixed a big piece of white paper over the whole blackboard, and the students watched. Then he brought his pen and on that big sheet of white paper he made just a small dot, a black dot — just a small one, barely visible. The students had to look very very closely, only then could they see it. And then he asked, "What do you see?" They all said, "A small dot." And nobody had seen the white paper — nobody, not a single student out of the fifty, said, "We see a big white sheet of paper over the whole blackboard." Not a single student said! They all said, "A black dot." And he had simply asked, "What do you see?"

What happened?! Emphasis. Continuously reading, you emphasize the dots, the black marks on the paper; you don't see the white paper.

Just change the emphasis. Start looking at the white paper rather than at the black dot — and that brings great revolution.

When two thoughts are moving in you, between the two thoughts there is a gap, an interval, a pause. When two words move in you, between these two words there is a gap again. Just look into the gaps more; become negligent of the words — look at the gaps.

Just standing on the road, try one experiment : you are standing on the road and cars are passing; maybe it is an international car rally and cars are passing. One car has gone, another car has gone, another car, but between two cars there are gaps... the road remains empty. Just change the emphasis! Just change the gestalt, as the Germans would like to say — change the gestalt, change the pattern.

Start looking between one gap and another gap. Rather than thinking one car has passed, another car has passed, another car has passed, start looking at the one gap that has passed, another gap, another gap — forget about the cars, start counting the gaps, how many gaps are passing. And you will be surprised — so many gaps are passing and you had never seen them before!

Just a change of emphasis : move from the figure to the background. Thoughts are figures, consciousness is the background. Mind consists of figures and no-mind is the background. Just start looking into the gaps. Fall in love with the intervals! Go deeper into them, search more into them — they have real secrets in them. The mystery is hidden there. It is not in the words that pass in your mind; those words are trivia, impressions from the outside. But see on what they pass, those ripples; look into that consciousness. And it is infinite. It is your being.

THAT consciousness is called no-mind.

That is the meaning of the English expression 'reading between the lines'. Read between the lines and you will become a wise man. Read the lines and you will become an ugly scholar, a pundit, a parrot, a computer, a memory — a mind. Read between the lines and you will become a no-mind.

And no-mind is herenow.

The second question :

You often say sannyas is to live in the utmost insecurity, but my experience has been different. I have felt more secure in my heart only since taking sannyas. What should I listen to? I am confused.

YOGA BHARTI, BOTH THINGS ARE TRUE — life is very paradoxical. I say to you : Sannyas is to live in utmost insecurity...

but the moment you start living in utmost insecurity, all insecurity disappears. Then you are secure for the first time.

Why does it happen?

The moment you accept insecurity, you stop asking for security. The moment you understand that insecurity is the nature of life, the moment you see that asking for security is asking for death... a secure person is a dead person. If you are alive you will have to live in insecurity.

Life is insecure, rooted in insecurity. One day you will have to die — how can you be secure? And you love a woman, and the woman is still alive — she can fall in love with somebody else. Nobody knows the ways of life — they are mysterious. And she is still alive; she is not dead. You can trust only a dead woman or a dead man.

That's why, the moment people fall in love they start killing each other — to create security. If you have killed the woman she becomes a wife; if you have killed the man he becomes a husband. Now you can be secure. There is security with a husband, but no life; and there is security with a wife, but no life. You have killed her so much that she cannot fall in love again. But remember : she cannot fall in love with anybody else — she cannot fall in love with you either. You have destroyed love.

You catch hold of a bird, and you had loved seeing it flying in the sky, it was so beautiful — it was freedom on wings. Now you are afraid : the bird may fly again. So you cut the wings and put him in a beautiful cage. Do you think it is the same bird that you had seen in the sky on the wing, whispering with the clouds? Do you think it is the same bird? It is a corpse, although it breathes. And it will never give you that joy.

That joy was not only because of the bird — many many things were involved in it... the open sky, the clouds, the sun, the wind. The FREEDOM was implied there! Now you have destroyed freedom, you have taken the sky away; you have taken the bird out of the WHOLE context. Now it has no meaning any more.

You see a beautiful flower on the rosebush and you cut it and you bring it home, and you put it on your table in a flowerpot — but it is no more the same flower. You have killed it! It is dying. And you will never see THAT beauty — because the juice was flowing, the flower was rooted in the earth. The earth was nourishing it and the sun was nourishing it and the wind was playing with it, and the fragrance was there... and all! You have taken it out of context. Now, in your plastic flowerpot you have encaged this beautiful flower, but it is dead.

That's what we go on doing.... You love a woman, and she was so alive — that's why! She was pure life. She was joy, she was dance, a song, and you had fallen in love with ALL those things together. Then you make a prisoner of her. You go to the court, you make legal conditions on her — you reduce her from the woman to a wife. This is an ugly phenomenon : to reduce any woman to a wife, to reduce any man to a husband. You have taken away ALL that was beautiful and glorious, all that was divine.

And now you are stuck with the woman and you wonder what has happened. Now you don't feel so much joy in her being. Now being with her is a tedium, a boredom. Have you not seen husbands and wives sitting together, how bored they look — utterly bored? If a friend comes or a neighbour, they start becoming a little alive; otherwise, they are utterly bored... looking into each other and finding nothing. They both have killed each other! And, naturally, they are angry too, because how can you forgive your murderer? You cannot.

The idea of security brings death in life. Afraid you may catch cold, you don't go into the rains. Afraid you may harm your body, you don't go to the playground. Afraid that you may fall from the tree, you don't climb. Afraid that death may happen, you don't go to the mountains. Afraid, afraid, afraid... you go on withdrawing yourself from life.

A moment comes — you are there but all life has disappeared. Then you are secure, but at what cost? And the more you make yourself secure, the more fear arises.

Have you not seen it? Poor people are less afraid than rich people — naturally, because they have much to lose, so more fear of insecurity. A rich man feels more insecure, because communism can come. What does a beggar bother about communism? He says, "Okay, let communism be! It doesn't matter." The rich man is always afraid the bank may fail, the business may fail... this may happen, that may happen. He is continuously worried.

It is not accidental that the rich man cannot sleep; the rich man suffers from insomnia. It is very rare to find a beggar suffering from insomnia; I have not found. I have been searching for a beggar who suffers from insomnia — I have not found. That is the rich man's disease. The beggar has nothing to worry about! He has nothing to LOSE! The rich man has a thousand and one things to worry about. He goes to bed, but the mind goes on spinning, weaving; it goes on working — a thousand and one things have to be settled, arranged, planned. Something may go wrong — how can he sleep? How can he afford sleep? A rich man is so poor, he cannot afford sleep; only a poor man is so rich that he can afford sleep.

Just watch how life functions : the more secure you become, the more afraid, frightened. And when you are more afraid, you want more security. When you have more security, you become more afraid... it is a vicious circle.

That's why I say sannyas is to live in utmost insecurity.

What do I mean by saying it? I mean that insecurity is life. There is no life without insecurity. That is the BEAUTY of life! that all can be lost. Hence the joy of the game. If it is certain that you will win, what will be the joy of it? If winning is certain, absolutely certain there cannot be any joy in it. The more uncertain the victory is, the more joy, the more search for it.

Life is insecure. This, when understood deeply, brings a kind of security — then you are no more afraid. Life IS insecure! You know perfectly well you have fallen in love with this woman and this woman can still fall in love, because she will still breathe, she will still be alive. Who knows about tomorrow? You are not the only man in the world. What foolishness to think that this woman cannot fall in love with anybody else! She CAN fall! And because she can fall, love her intensely — because who knows about tomorrow? Tomorrow she may go and may not turn again and may not see you again. This may be your last time — make as much of it as you can.

This is the understanding of sannyas, that tomorrow is not certain, only this moment is my moment — I have to live it in totality.

And I am not saying that she WILL leave you, or she has to leave you. In fact, if you love her totally in this moment, how can she leave you? If you have loved her so much, how can she leave you? Out of today will come tomorrow. Out of this moment will follow the next. If this moment has been of such ecstasy, how can she leave you? Out of insecurity, security is born — she cannot leave you. It is impossible to leave you — not because of the law and the court and the marriage and the society, but just because you loved her so much.

You have given her the first insight into no-time, no-mind. You have been a door to the divine — how can she leave you? She has already become part of you; you have become part of her. But this is happening of its own; it is unmanaged. Out of insecurity you loved her totally, and out of total love life becomes secure.

So, Bharti, you are right — what I say is true, what you feel is true too. Sannyas is uttermost insecurity, and once you are a sannyasin you start having a new vision of life. And that new vision KNOWS NOTHING OF INSECURITY.

Because it is such a paradox, the problem arises : WHAT SHOULD I LISTEN TO? I AM CONFUSED.

You need not be confused. Always remember : anything, to be true, has to be paradoxical. Truth is paradoxical. Only lies are not paradoxical. Whenever you see that something is not paradoxical, beware! — there must be some lie.

Truth IS paradox. That is an absolute quality of truth.

What is desirelessness? Is it to be totally without desire or to be totally free to have or not have desire?

TO BE TOTALLY FREE OF DESIRE WILL MAKE YOU DEAD — you will not be alive any more. That's what has been taught : Be desireless! But what can you do? You can go on cutting desires; the more desires are cut, the poorer your life becomes. If all desires are destroyed, then you have committed suicide, spiritual suicide.

No, desire is the energy of life, desire is life. Then what DO I mean when I say be free of desire?

The second is my meaning : to be free, totally free, to have or not have desire. Desire should not be an obsession — that is the meaning. You should be capable... for example, you see somebody's beautiful house, newly built, and a desire arises in you to have such a house. Now, are you free to have this desire or not? If you are free, I will say you are desireless. If you say, "I am not free. This desire persists. Even if I want to drop it, I cannot drop it — it haunts me. I see dreams of that house, I think about it. I am afraid to go on that road, because that house creates jealousy in me, that house creates disturbance in me." If you say, "I am not capable of either having or not having the desire," then you are not in a healthy shape — then desires are your masters, you are a victim. And you will suffer much because there are millions of things going around, and if so many desires take possession of you, you will be torn apart.

That's how it is happening : somebody has become the prime minister, now YOU want to become the prime minister; somebody has become very rich, now you want to become very rich; somebody has become a famous writer, now you want to become a famous writer. And somebody is something else... and somebody is something else... and all around there are millions of people doing millions of things. And from every nook and corner a desire arises and jumps on you and takes possession of you, and if you are not capable of saying yes or no you will go mad.

That's how the whole of humanity is mad. All those desires are pulling you into so many directions. You have become fragmentary, because many desires have possessed parts of your being.

AND those desires are contradictory too. Then it is not only that you are fragmentary : you become a contradiction. One part of you wants to become very rich, another part of you wants to become a poet — now, this is difficult. It is very difficult to become rich and remain a poet. A poet cannot be that cruel; it will be very difficult for him to become rich.

Money is not poetry : money is blood, money is exploitation. A poet worth the name cannot exploit. And a poet worth the name will have some vision of beauty. He cannot be so ugly himself as to deprive so many people just for his desire to hoard money.

Now, you want to become a politician, and you also want to meditate; you want to become a meditator too. This is not possible. Politicians cannot be religious. They can pretend to be religious, but they cannot be religious. How can a politician be religious? — because religion means non-ambitiousness and politics is nothing but pure ambition.

Religiousness means : I am happy as I am. Politics means : I will be happy only when I am at the top — I am not happy as I am. I have to run and rush, and I will destroy if it is needed. If by right means, okay; if not, then by wrong means — but I have to be at the top, I have to prove myself.

A politician naturally suffers from an inferiority complex. A religious man has no complex — inferiority or superiority.

Politicians pretend to be religious because that pays in politics. Morarji Desai pretends to be religious — that pays in politics. Now, look at the disgusting thing Jimmy Carter has done : he came to India and he asked, first thing in India, three hours for prayer. He knows India is a religious country — three hours for prayer?! Prayer is nothing to be bragged about. You can do it in your bedroom — three minutes are enough — three seconds are enough — just a single moment is enough — because prayer has nothing to do with time : it needs intensity. Now, a three-hour prayer! think of God also a little bit : listening to Jimmy Carter for three hours... poor old man! Nobody thinks of God. And what will you be saying for three hours? You will bore Him to death! But he knows that India is a religious country, people will be impressed by the idea.

And what can Jimmy Carter do for three hours, what will he pray for three hours? A politician cannot pray even for three minutes; he will be thinking all the time about politics.

To be religious means to be non-ambitious, to have no ambitions of being somewhere else, somebody else — to be herenow!

Now, if you have these two ideas together, that you want to be a politician and you also want to be a meditator, you will be in difficulty — you will drive yourself crazy. If you are honest, you will go mad; if you are dishonest, then you will not go mad — then you will become a hypocrite. That's what your politicians are.

And I am not saying that all those who are in religion are not politicians : out of a hundred there are also ninety-nine who are politicians. They are there in a different kind of politics : the religious politics. They have THEIR hierarchy and the priest wants to become the Pope — again it is politics. Or, the sinner wants to become the saint — again it is politics, again it is inferiority complex; again, once you have started doing something holy, religious, saintly, you will carry around yourself that ego of 'holier than thou'. Then you will have a condemnation of others in your eyes; then everybody is doomed and only you are going to be saved. Then you can look at others with pity : These people are going to hell.

This is again politics.

A religious man knows no ego. He is not even humble — remember — he is so egoless he is not even humble. Humbleness is also a pretension of ego; the humble person is also TRYING to be humble and trying to prove that "I am humble"; or even may have ideas deep inside his heart that "I am the MOST humble man in the world." Again it is the ego!

Many desires will take possession of you and many will be contradictory and you will be pulled apart and you will start falling into pieces, you will lose integrity, you will no more be an individual.

You ask : WHAT IS DESIRELESSNESS?

Now, these are the two things : you know desirelessness, then you have to cut your life completely, then everything has to be cut. Then you become a Jain monk — just an empty shell utterly discontented with everything, with yourself; uncreative, no celebration, no flowers ever bloom. Or you know desirefulness : then you become torn apart. Both are ugly states.

The right thing to do is to be so totally free from desire that you can choose, that you are always able to choose : to have or not to have. Then you are really free. And then you will have both the creativity, the celebration, the joy of desires, AND the silence and the peace and the calmness of desirelessness.

The fourth question :

Beloved master, I know we are not the body, or the 'cloud' as you called it... But when I open my eyes I can't help noticing that your toes are turning blue from the cold! Why won't you wear a wrap or a shawl, or why won't you let us put a quilt or something over your legs?

THIS QUESTION IS FROM DIVYA — but there are four other questions similar, all from women sannyasins : Pradeepa, Gyan Bhakti, Krishna Priya.

Thank you, but you don't know anything about my toes — they enjoy cold like anything. I understand your sympathy, but from my very childhood I have enjoyed cold like anything. Just as you enjoy ice-cream my toes enjoy cold. Don't feel sorry for them — they are very happy.

The fifth question :

You always speak so beautifully of creativity and aesthetics...! Will there be work for poets, painters, sculptors, designers, musicians, craftsmen, etc. at the new commune?

YES, KATYAYANI — art is going to be the religion of the new commune.

And the sixth question :

I do not trust your words. At first I could grab on to a phrase or a theme and hug it to my bosom — paste it on my wall — repeat it as a mantram — aha! Now I have a key — but the next day or the next week you say the opposite.

Now I am afraid to listen to you.

THAT IS THE WHOLE PURPOSE OF LISTENING TO ME : so that you don't become a hoarder, so that no thought becomes so important to you that it takes possession of you.

I would like you to become a no-mind. And those phrases, howsoever beautiful they are, if you hug them to the bosom and paste them on the wall and repeat them as a mantram, they will create mind.

That's why I have to go on destroying myself. I say one thing, and before you can hoard it, I destroy it. I will do it so continuously, so consistently, that sooner or later you will not hug any phrase to your heart, and you will not paste any phrase on your wall, and you will NOT take ANYTHING as a mantram!

That day, Amida, will be a great day of liberation for you. Then you will simply listen as you listen to music. Why can't you listen to me as you listen to music? Why listen to me with a business mind, with some purpose in it? Why jump upon things and start collecting them? Why not listen simply, innocently, without catching hold of anything? Listen just as you listen to music, and that will be far more enriching. Then mind will not be nourished.

And my work here is to destroy your mind, so that your no-mind becomes available to you.

The seventh question :

What is a question? And is there an answer to every question? And why do you answer our questions?

A QUESTION IS A MISUNDERSTANDING. You have misunderstood life as a problem — hence questions arise. Life is not a problem : life is a mystery.

But the misunderstanding is possible because a mystery looks like a problem, a mystery looks like a riddle — and the ego starts trying to solve it. Hence the question. But a mystery means a mystery — it is a riddle which cannot be solved. A mystery is by its very definition insoluble. So ALL questions are irrelevant.

And when questions are irrelevant, naturally answers are also irrelevant. A question is a misunderstanding about life : you think it can be solved — this is the misunderstanding. Nobody has ever solved anything. Great philosophies have been evolved, but not a single question has been answered ever.

One can BELIEVE that one has got the answer, but that is just a belief. Just look a little bit more and you will find that your answer was just a make-believe.

There are no answers.

All questions are meaningless.

But then the question arises : AND IS THERE AN ANSWER TO EVERY QUESTION?

There is not a single question which can be answered. Small questions : What is yellow? — cannot be answered. All your science and all your philosophy and all your religions cannot answer a simple, silly question : What is yellow? How can you answer it?!

A great philosopher, G.E. Moore, has written a book *Principia Ethica*. In two hundred pages he goes on asking one question only : What is good? And he was one of the most important philosophers of this century and one of the most logical minds. You cannot improve upon Moore. And he asks a simple question : What is good? And he asks in a thousand ways, and answers and answers and answers... and finally, in the end, he says : The good is indefinable.

It is like yellow — what is yellow?

All philosophies have failed.

So it is not that there are questions which can be answered and there are a few questions which cannot be answered — not a single question can be answered. Questioning is a wrong approach towards reality. You question : you go wrong.

Then, naturally, you ask : AND WHY DO YOU ANSWER OUR QUESTIONS? — if no question can be answered, then why do I go on answering you?

Just to help you know that no questions can be answered. Just to destroy your questions — not to answer but to destroy.

Watch my answers! They are not really answers to your questions — they are just like hammers. I try to destroy your questions — sometimes politely and sometimes not so politely. But the whole effort is to destroy the question.

Naturally, I destroy one, you produce another — then I have

to destroy that. This is the fight between a Master and a disciple. It goes on and on. But the disciple has always been defeated.

How long can you go on asking? Many of you have stopped asking, but new people go on coming so the story continues. One day, all of you will have stopped — stopping, not out of defeat, not out of desperation, but out of understanding. Seeing the point, that life is a mystery to be lived, not a problem to be solved — that is metanoia. You are converted. You have moved from mind to no-mind.

And the last question :

This crazy, sweet, totally demanding and physically exhausting, delightful marathon called motherhood... since this fireball came to us — almost two years now — not one uninterrupted night's sleep, not one day of rest. And feeling nothing so important as simply being present for him — and so very often inadequate and tense and tired in that.

Where is laughter in this?

Help! Help! Yuck, Yuck, Yuck.

Yet another 'Jewish Mother'

Ma Prem Punita

PUNITA, JUST TO GIVE BIRTH TO A CHILD IS ONE THING — to be a mother is totally different. Any woman can give birth to a child; that's a very simple phenomenon. But to be a mother needs great art, needs great understanding.

You are creating a human being — that is the greatest creation! A painter paints a picture; we call it great art. Picasso — we call him a great artist. But what about the mother who created Picasso? A poet writes beautiful poems, but what about the mother who created Shakespeare? We don't think about mothers as the greatest creative people on the earth.

That is one of the reasons why women are not great painters and great poets — they need not be : they can be great mothers. Why does man try to become a great scientist, poet, painter, this and that? — he is jealous of women : he cannot create children. He feels impotent.

Sigmund Freud has talked much about phallic jealousy —that women suffer from a jealousy because they don't have penises. Now this is utterly meaningless, absurd. It is as if a woman Sigmund Freud is born and starts talking about men suffering from breast-jealousy because they don't have breasts.

But, one thing is certain : deep down man always feels jealous that he cannot mother, that he cannot carry an alive life in him, that he cannot reproduce life. To substitute it he paints, he sculpts, he writes poetry, he composes music; he goes to the moon, he goes to Everest. He wants to prove at least to his woman that "I can also do something," otherwise he feels impotent. Compared to woman's capacity, he looks like a child, looks almost accidental. His work is not much : giving birth to a child, he simply triggers the process. A small injection can do that; that is not much of a work.

The woman passes through those nine months of agony and ecstasy. And then the work is not finished! In fact, then the work, the real work, starts — when the child is born. And the child brings again a fresh quality to life. Every child is primitive, a barbarian; now the mother has to civilize. Every child is a barbarian, remember; he is animal, wild. And the mother has to give him culture, has to teach him the ways of life, the ways of man. It is a great work.

Punita, you have to remember that — that your work has not finished, it has started. Take it joyously! You are creating something immensely valuable — you are carving a life, you are protecting a life. The work is such that no sacrifice is great enough for it — any sacrifice can and should be made. One thing.

Second thing : don't take it too seriously, otherwise you will destroy the child. Your seriousness will become destructive. Take it playfully. The responsibility is there! but it has to be taken very playfully. Play upon the child as one plays upon a musical instrument — and she knows how to play on musical instruments. Let the child be your instrument now. Play carefully but play playfully. If you become serious, then the child will start feeling your seriousness and the child will be crushed and crippled. Don't burden the child; don't start feeling that you are doing something great to the child. When I say you are doing something great, you are doing something great to YOURSELF. By helping this child to grow into a beautiful human being, into a Buddha, you will be becoming the mother of a Buddha. You will not be obliging the child : you will be simply enjoying your own life; your own life will become a fragrance through the child.

This is an opportunity, a God-given opportunity.

And these are the two pitfalls : either you neglect the child, you are tired of it; or you become too serious about the child, and you start burdening him, obliging him. Both are wrong. Help the child — but for the sheer joy of it. And never feel that he owes any debt to you. On the contrary, feel thankful that he has chosen you to be his mother. Let your motherhood bloom through him.

If you can bloom into your motherhood, you will feel thankful to the child forever.

And, naturally, there will be sacrifices, but they have to be made... joyously. Only then is it a sacrifice! If you DO it without joy it is not sacrifice. Sacrifice comes from the word 'sacred'. When you do it joyfully, it is sacred. When you don't do it joyfully, then you are just fulfilling a duty — and all duties are ugly, they are not sacred.

This is a great opportunity. Meditate over it, go into it deeply. You will never find such a deep involvement —in fact, there is none AS it is between a child and the mother. Not even between the husband and the wife, the lover and the beloved — the involvement is not so deep as it is between the mother and the child. It can NOT be so deep with anybody ever — because the child has lived in you for nine months as you; nobody else can live in you for nine months as you.

And the child will become a separate individual sooner or later, but somewhere deep down in the unconscious the mother and the child remain linked.

If your child can become a Buddha, you will be benefited by it; if your child grows and becomes a beautiful human being, you will be benefited by it — because the child will always remain connected with you. Only the physical connection has been disconnected; the spiritual connection is never disconnected.

Thank God! Motherhood is a blessing.

CHAPTER
4

I Am Happening To You

The first question :

Listening to you in the discourse, it is the pauses, the gaps, between two sentences, two words, that roll in my ears like thunder, tearing me open and tearing me apart.

I am being taken to a space beyond tears or laughter by your silence. What is happening to me?

*P*REM DAS — I AM HAPPENING TO YOU. ALLOW IT. Sometimes it will be frightening, scary, because you will be going into spaces you are not acquainted with.

You will be moving beyond yourself. You will be entering into the unknown. And the unknown is always frightening. The new always creates great fear. With the old, one feels perfectly comfortable. The old always feels cozy, snug. With the new, you have to learn again. With the new you have to become a child again. The new happens only to those who are ready to become children again and again and again — because the old knowledge, the old experience, the old life, will have no meaning in the new. It will be irrelevant. You will suddenly feel ignorant facing the unknown.

Hence the fear! Hence the clinging to the past.

Remember : the journey to truth is a journey from the old to the new, from the known to the unknown, from the closed to the open. And I can happen to you only in the pauses.

Words are used to create the pauses — not vice versa. I am saying things and talking to you just to give you an experience of silence. Those pauses are the most significant thing that is being delivered to you, being transferred to you. Be available in those pauses.

They will tear you apart. They will destroy you. That's why I say I have come to destroy, not to fulfill. But remember : the ONLY way to fulfillment is through destruction. If you are destroyed utterly, only then will you be utterly new. Through crucifixion is resurrection.

Let me first become your crucifixion. Let me first become your cross. And then the second thing follows naturally... nothing has to be done about it. To die is to be reborn.

Die in those pauses, in those silences, in those gaps! In those gaps, MY meditativeness is flowing towards you — receive it. Receive it with great joy. Receive it as you would receive a guest, a cherished guest. Open the doors of your heart.

And, yes, there will be great chaos with it — I will bring chaos in you — but that is the only way stars are born : out of chaos. I will bring great upheavals in your being, I will uproot you from where you are, because that is the only way to transform, to transplant you onto higher plenitudes of being. And there are higher and higher plenitudes, there is no end to it. This is an eternal pilgrimage.

I know fear is natural! But don't get caught by it. Leave it aside. Move in spite of it.

Always remember : the difference between a courageous man and a coward is not that the courageous man has no fear and the coward has fear — no. That is not the difference. BOTH have fear! in the SAME proportion. Then where is the difference? The difference is that the courageous man goes in spite of the fear, and the coward stops because of the fear. Both have fears!

If you can find a courageous man who has no fear, then how will you call him courageous? He will be a machine, not a man. Only machines don't have fear. But you don't call machines courageous. How can you call a machine courageous? Courage simply means that something is happening in spite of the fear. The fear is there, the trembling is there, but it is not stopping you, you are not being blocked by it. You use it as a stepping-stone. Shaking, trembling, but still you go into the unknown.

To be a sannyasin is to choose courage.

Both possibilities exist in every human being! fear and courage. All will depend on which you choose between the two. Never choose fear. It cripples. It paralyzes. It destroys you without giving you a chance of resurrection. Courage will ALSO destroy you, but that destruction is very creative — it will give you rebirth.

Fear and courage, both destroy — but fear simply destroys. The seed simply goes rotten. When you sow the seed of courage in the soil, then too it dies — but it doesn't go rotten. It dies... it dies into a new phenomenon. A sprout comes up.

Courage will kill you as much as fear, but fear will simply kill you without giving you a new life. Courage will give you a new life. Choose courage — always choose courage.

Arduous it is, but it is adventurous too. Difficult it is, uncomfortable, inconvenient it is, but it brings great ecstasies too. One has to pay the price for those ecstasies.

The second question:

If my mind still controls and blocks my feelings, how do I discover what is the next appropriate step for me to take?

LISTEN TO THIS QUESTION AGAIN, very carefully: IF.... It is not a true question; it starts with 'if'. It is as if you are asking a hypothetical thing. You are supposing a question.

Never ask such questions. At least be honest about your questions. If they ARE there, then ask. And I know the question is there, but you don't even want to take the responsibility for it. The question is valid — but you start by an 'if'? Can't you say that "this is my problem"? You want it to appear theoretical? You want it to appear impersonal? Then you will miss the answer — because I don't give answers to theoretical questions.

This is not a philosophy class — I am not teaching you philosophy — I am teaching you life. NOT a philosophy of life, but life itself.

Remember: when you ask a question, let it be true. Don't camouflage it, don't cover it. Don't try to be clever with me, otherwise you will be at a loss.

It may have happened unconsciously; I am not saying that you have put that 'if' consciously. You are not that conscious, I know. It must have happened mechanically. You may have learnt the trick of how to ask questions —and remain aloof, and detached, and out of them.

This is not the way to write or ask a question! — with me at least. You have to be in your question. I am going to be in my answer, and if you are not in your question, where and how shall we meet? If I am in my answer, I am absolutely there.

You have to be in your question — only then is the meeting possible. And the meeting is the solution — not the answer, not the question : the meeting. The point where my consciousness touches your consciousness. But if you are not in your question and I answer it, how am I going to touch your consciousness? You will be absent! I will be knocking on a door where you are not.

Don't be so much afraid of the answer. Be authentic. Be existential! Let the question have the flavour of your being! Let the question have a LIFE — it should have a heart which beats, it should BREATHE! Then only is there some possibility....

You kill the question from the very beginning : 'if'?

IF MY MIND STILL CONTROLS... as if it is not controlling and you are asking for others' sake.

IF MY MIND STILL CONTROLS... and just watch how many times in such a small sentence 'I', 'my', 'mine', have come.

IF my MIND STILL CONTROLS AND BLOCKS MY FEELINGS, HOW DO I DISCOVER WHAT IS THE NEXT APPROPRIATE STEP FOR ME TO TAKE?

With so much 'I', whatever step you take will be wrong. With so much 'I', a right step cannot be taken at all. The 'I' is the poison. It will destroy whatsoever you do.

With so much 'I', if you love, your love will turn into hatred. With so much 'I', if you meditate, your meditation will be nothing but a madness inside. With so much 'I', if you look at the flowers, you will not see the beauty.

I Am Happening To You 〜 **73**

The 'I' IS ugly, and it creates ugliness all around it.

In fact, the very question :... WHAT IS THE NEXT APPROPRIATE STEP? is because of the 'I'. The 'I' wants to control not only THIS step but the next too. It has been controlling all your past steps, it is controlling your present step, it wants to control the next step too. What do you mean by APPROPRIATE? That which fits with your ideas of right, true; that which fits with your idea of religion, spirituality. And what do you know of religion and spirituality? What do you know of truth? How can your next step be adequate? appropriate?

Any step which is in accordance with the truth, any step which has the quality of suchness in it, is appropriate. But what do you know about suchness? You have lived in the mind — with the 'I', 'me', 'mine'. All that you know is just rubbish. And out of that rubbish, you want to take an appropriate step? Remember : out of mind there is no appropriate step; out of mind all steps are inappropriate. Why? What do I mean when I say that?

Let us move slowly into this phenomenon.

Life brings a situation. Those situations are always new. Life is immensely creative; it never repeats. Even if you feel it is a repetition, it is not. There are vital differences, subtle differences... may not be available to you on the surface, but have you seen two mornings exactly the same? Have you ever come across two roseflowers exactly the same? Have you come across two human beings exactly the same? What to say about human beings? — you cannot find two pebbles exactly the same. You can search the whole earth....

Life is always fresh. That is the MEANING of being alive — life is always moving into new spaces. And your mind is always old; it knows nothing of the new. It knows only of the past. It knows only of that which has happened. It accumulates experiences. 'Experience' means it has happened. And remember : life is never going to repeat the same situation in which that experience happened. And you act out of the mind, hence there is always a gap between you and life — and nothing is appropriate. How can it be appropriate?

You act out of the past experiences and life is always creating new spaces. You never meet with life, you never merge with life. You are always inappropriate. Your answers don't fit the questions that life raises. Your responses are not responses but reactions.

To be appropriate means to me to be spontaneous. Not to act out of the mind is to be appropriate : to act in THIS moment, to act utterly in this moment, to see the situation and to act, respond to the situation.

Don't search in your memory for what is appropriate, because the memory will supply you with answers which are NOT appropriate and cannot be appropriate. The memory is always irrelevant. You have to put the memory aside. You have to be in a kind of absolute exposure to the reality, to the situation that is.

And let your total being respond. Don't decide about it. Don't rehearse it. Don't prepare for it. Let it respond! And then it will be appropriate.

When YOU are not, it will be appropriate. When the mind is not brought in, it will be appropriate. When it is spontaneous, it will be appropriate. Bring a little preparation in it, just a little bit, and you have poisoned it, then it is never appropriate.

Life is not a school examination where you go prepared. That's why schools are so ugly — they don't prepare you for life, they destroy all possibilities of life. Schools have to disappear from the world, and the colleges and the universities. They are anti-life. They believe in rehearsals. They believe in giving you fixed answers — as if there are fixed challenges! — the basic fallacy.

And one third of the life is wasted in the university. By the time you are ready with a Ph.D. one third of the life has gone down the drain. And what are you ready for? You have simply bookish answers crammed into your head; you have become a computer. And now, with all that knowledge, whatsoever you do will be INAPPROPRIATE!

A knowledgeable man has never been known to be appropriate — never. He always goes on missing the train; he is always late. He is never to the point — he cannot be. His arrows never reach the target — they cannot reach, because the target is moving! and his ideas of it are fixed.

Education no longer prepares you for life : it prepares you for death. Your universities are cemeteries where the past lives and goes on killing the present — and the future too. Education, as it is in the world now, is very reactionary. A totally different kind of education is needed — not that which simply goes on helping you to cram answers, but that which helps you to be open, which helps you to function from a state of not knowing.

Mm? — that's what meditation is all about : a state of not knowing. Then whatsoever you do is going to be appropriate, because then you are no more the doer —then God is the doer. Then life itself is responding.

Just try to observe a few moments when you are spontaneous — they will give you such joy.

For example : somebody is drowning in the river, and you stand there and you think about it — "What should I do? What is appropriate?" If you are a Christian missionary, you will think this is a great opportunity to help and serve humanity — this is a way to reach heaven and be special there. And you repeat in your head all the quotes from the Bible, what Jesus has said — that service is the way to God... and you jump! You are not concerned with this poor human being who is drowning : you are concerned with your ego trip you call spirituality. You want to be virtuous.

This is so ugly! This spirituality, this religiousness, this service, is so ugly. It is not a spontaneous act, it is not out of your heart — it is out of your head.

And if your head has been prepared in a different way, for example, if you had been born in another religion... there exists a religion in India, a sect of Jains — Terapanth : if you had been born into that sect, then these ideas wouldn't come to you. A follower of Terapanth will stand there on the bank, he will also think just like you are thinking, but he will think... his scriptures say : Everybody suffers according to his karmas. Now, this man is drowning, he must have done some bad karmas in the past. And his scriptures say : Don't come in the way of anybody's karmas. Now, he is being punished by his own karmas — you need not jump and save him. That will not be a help; you will be hindering, you will be delaying! If you get him out of the river and you save him, some day he will again have to fall into the river and drown. Mm? the mathematics of karma : he HAS to. Maybe he killed his wife in some past life by drowning her in water — now he HAS to suffer!

Now think! From these two different minds : the Christian thinks this is the opportunity to go to God and the Jain thinks this is the opportunity not to get emotional — mm? — this is foolish to jump; it is emotional, sentimental. He has to control himself not to jump and not to save this human being, because he is suffering his karmas — let him suffer so that he can be finished with it. Next life he will be born in a better life, in a better way.

Now both these people are acting out of their memories. Can't you see a third possibility : just acting out of the spontaneity of the moment, on the spur of the moment — neither a Hindu, nor a Christian, nor a Mohammedan, nor a Jain, nor a Buddhist... nobody? Just acting out of the situation itself? Then it is appropriate.

That is my definition of 'appropriate'. Act out of the mind and it is inappropriate; it is not true to the situation. Act without mind and it is appropriate.

Now I will read the question again :

IF MY MIND STILL CONTROLS AND BLOCKS MY FEELINGS, HOW DO I DISCOVER WHAT IS THE NEXT APPROPRIATE STEP FOR ME TO TAKE?

Don't think of the morrow. Just be in this moment, spontaneous, and out of the spontaneity of this moment the spontaneity of the next will follow of its own accord. You are not to plan for it.

But we have become great planners. You come from the office and you start planning on the way what your wife will ask and how you will answer, and you prepare everything. You go to the office from the house and you know what your boss is going to say and what you are going to answer.

You go on preparing! You don't trust life.

To trust life is to be appropriate. What do I mean by trusting life? I mean let the moment come... let it happen... you be there present... you be available! And then whatsoever happens through you is good, is virtue.

Virtue is not a decision on your part. Sin is a decision on your part. Whatsoever you decide becomes a sin. The word 'decision' is beautiful. It is made of two words : 'de', 'cision' — it means 'cut off'. Every decision cuts you off from life. When you act out of decisions, you act against life. When you allow life to take possession of you, everything is appropriate.

The third question :

I am gathering courage to ask this question. No Buddha ever hung his picture round the neck of his disciples —yet you are doing it. Is there any purpose behind it?

MOHAN BHARTI, EVERY BUDDHA HAS HIS OWN ECCENTRICITIES AND CRAZINESSES — this is mine! And I am not supposed to repeat anybody else's eccentricities — I can have my own.

And remember : there is no purpose behind it — there is no purpose behind ANY of my activities here! It is just to make you a fool, that's all — so that when you go into the world, you look ridiculous.

The fourth question :

You have said not to condition children with our ideas. What about sannyasin children? Why not let them choose consciously whether and when to take sannyas? For example, for children living in the West — outside of the ashram anyway — cannot the fact of their being sannyasins condition them in their relationship to other children or to their environment?

DEVA MAJID, CAN I ASK YOU A QUESTION? — Have you taken sannyas consciously? Who has taken sannyas consciously? If you are conscious, then what is the need, in fact, of taking sannyas? In that way, everybody is the same as children, grown-up, makes no difference.

Children are truer. It often happens : a sannyasin mother or father brings a child to take sannyas and he falls asleep — and that is the true picture of a sannyasin! But he is authentic and you keep your eyes open, that's the only difference. You are fast asleep with open eyes and the child is true : he is asleep so he has closed his eyes — that's all. Why keep your eyes open when you are asleep? What is the point of it?

The only difference I see between you and the children is that you are asleep with open eyes, unnecessarily straining your eyes, and the child is perfectly at ease.

Sometimes it happens : I give sannyas to children when they are snoring but that is my experience with you too. So I don't see the point, why they should be prevented. If they are to be prevented from sannyas, then EVERYBODY has to be prevented. And if you are not prevented, then why be hard on children?

Sannyas is just an initiation towards consciousness. It can't be expected from you that you should be conscious when you take sannyas.

Sannyas is medicinal. When you are ill, medicine is needed. If a doctor makes it a condition that "Come only when you are healthy — I am not going to pour my medicine into such an ill body. First get healthy and then come," then what is the point? Sannyas is medicinal — because you are unconscious, it is needed. I cannot expect you to take sannyas consciously; that is impossible. If you can take sannyas consciously, then you can do ANYTHING consciously. Then what is the problem? If you can take sannyas consciously, why can't you eat consciously? Why can't you walk consciously? Why can't you love consciously? Where is the problem then? Then you will be conscious! You will be a Buddha and sannyas will not be needed.

You cannot be conscious, that's why sannyas is needed. Sannyas is a beginning, not an end — first thing.

Second thing : the question is — YOU HAVE SAID NOT TO CONDITION CHILDREN.... Sannyas is a process of unconditioning, remember it. It is not a process of conditioning : it is a process of unconditioning.

What am I doing here? I am not giving you knowledge — I am taking your knowledge away. It is a kind of mind-wash. I am simply cleaning your mind, effacing things, taking your ideas, helping you to drop those stupid fixations. I am not giving you anything as a substitute for them! You would like that very much.

People come to me, they say, "But give us some philosophy to live for!" Life is enough! What do you need a philosophy to live for? Life in itself is more than enough. They say, "That's right — but something to live for, something to hope for, something for inspiration" — something so that they can plan, so that they can destroy the future, so that they can stop being spontaneous.

People ask me, "Some discipline is needed" — particularly religious people, when they come to me they are very much shocked that I don't give any particular discipline to sannyasins. Do you think wearing orange is a discipline? or having the mala around your neck is a discipline? or the change of your name is a discipline? Do you think these are disciplines? These are games! These are not disciplines!

Discipline is when you move into a Christian monastery.

Discipline is when you become a Jain monk — then what to eat, what not to eat, how much to eat, when to go to sleep, how much to sleep, then a twenty-four-hour programme is given to you. Sooner or later you become a robot, you become just a machine — a perfect machine; efficient, but a machine. You are no more human beings.

I am not giving you any discipline. I give you only awareness — because to me awareness is the fundamental thing. If you are aware, you will find your discipline yourself. Who am I to give it to you?

And ANY fixed discipline will create problems — it will be inappropriate. How can you decide for tomorrow? And when you have a character, you have decided for tomorrow — that is the meaning of character. That's why in society people who have character are respected, because they are predictable people, you can rely upon them. You know that this man NEVER speaks a lie; he can be used in business — you can rely upon him, he will never speak a lie — he has character. This man will not steal — he has character; you can rely on him, otherwise he will take your money. This man will not start an affair with your wife — he has character. You can rely on him; he can be allowed to remain in your house and work. This man will not suddenly jump upon you and kill you — you can rely on him, he has character. He has never done anything like that. He has certificates.

A man of character simply means one whose past is so fixed that you can rely on it that he will not be able to change it in the future either.

I don't give you any discipline, any character. My basic approach is that one has to be utterly characterless! To be characterless means to be without the past. I am not saying that you have to commit murder and you have to start stealing and robbing people — I am not saying that. But I am saying this : that you should not be predictable like a man of character.

Yes, you will not commit murder — not because it is your character but because of your awareness you cannot do such an ugly thing. Not because it is against the Ten Commandments and

Moses and Manu and Mahavir, no — but because your inner voice is against it. You will not rob anybody, not because it is written in the scriptures that you will suffer in hell, but because the very idea does not arise in a conscious mind.

A conscious mind has a fluid discipline about it, but fluid — it changes according to circumstances.

A man of character is like one who goes out to the market and it starts raining but he will not open his umbrella because he has never opened it before — he is a man of character. But my sannyasin will open the umbrella! and when it stops raining will close the umbrella. The umbrella is to be USED; it is not a fixation. When it is too hot, you move inside the house, you seek coolness. When it is too cool and getting cold in the house, you start moving outside to seek the sun's warmth.

Life should be fluid, natural. That's what sannyas is : it is an unconditioning. It takes your character, your knowledge, your past — you — away from you. It makes you fluid. It helps you to melt. It is unconditioning.

You ask : YOU HAVE SAID NOT TO CONDITION CHILDREN.

Yes, don't condition them — and sannyas is a way to protect them from conditioning.

YOU HAVE SAID NOT TO CONDITION CHILDREN WITH OUR IDEAS.

SANNYAS IS NOT AN IDEA. It is a device. It is a method, not an idea. Just by becoming a sannyasin, you stop being a Christian, a Jew, a Hindu, a Buddhist. Just by becoming a sannyasin, you stop being an American, an Indian, a Japanese, a German — these are ugly boundaries. They are not any more valuable than what dogs do — they urinate and make a boundary, and that becomes their territory. These national boundaries are nothing but dog boundaries made by urinating. Ugly they are.

By becoming a sannyasin you become a citizen of the earth —

you are no more an Indian, no more a Tibetan, no more a Chinese. You claim the whole earth, and that is the beginning of claiming the whole universe. Passports are ugly, visas are ugly. They simply show that the world is not yet free. They simply show that there is NO freedom of movement in this world, that you cannot enter a country freely, that there are a thousand and one obstructions, that you cannot choose your country freely, that this whole earth is not available to you, that these nations are nothing but big prisons. Inside you are allowed to move, but outside you are not allowed to move. This is ugly.

A sannyasin is a world citizen. Sannyas is the beginning of a new concept of consciousness, that we are all one. This may be the only place on the earth where nobody bothers who is a Jain, who is a Hindu, who is a Mohammedan....

I was worried about my old parents when they came and stayed here — I was worried that it would be too much for them. But I was very happy when they went to take their meals with Krishna Mohammed and Radha — I was so happy! That was a great step! Otherwise, they are orthodox Jains.

In my childhood I HAD a Mohammedan friend. It was very difficult for me to invite him some time for tea or for food, very difficult. And even if I would insist, my family would allow, but then we would have to sit outside the house to eat, because the Mohammedan cannot sit inside. And when I insisted again and again, then they had to prepare separate pots and things for my friend. They were kept only for him; nobody else would touch them.

The world has lived like that, with a thousand and one divisions — of religion, of sect, of politics. To be a sannyasin means you are dropping all divisions. You are declaring humanity is one, and this whole planet belongs to us. This is our home.

And when we have a really great number of sannyasins roaming around the world, then many things can become possible. It depends. If we have enough numbers of sannyasins around the world, it can usher a new era. Passports should be dropped some day, visas should be dropped some day. We should declare that we are free to move! Nobody can prevent us! We are free to live wherever we want. And the freedom of movement is one of the basic freedoms.

Why are nations so much afraid? Why so many visas and passports and boundaries and borders? There are very very deep reasons you may not be aware of. In fact, the traveller is a dangerous phenomenon for closed societies. Why? Because the traveller brings new concepts of life; his existence is disruptive to the orthodox, to the conventional.

For example, my sannyasins moving in India are a problem. What is the problem? They don't do any harm to anybody.

Just the other day, a couple was just holding hands outside the ashram — not doing anything! — just sitting silently holding hands, and a man jumped upon them and started shouting and abusing : "You are destroying our Hindu culture! I don't allow my children to come in Koregaon Park, because if they see you people they will be destroyed."

I would like my sannyasins to roam around the earth as much as possible, to destroy children, to destroy these chauvinists — Hindu, Christian, Mohammedan — it doesn't matter who they are. Roam around the earth, be mobile, and with you the fragrance will spread.

That's why Russia does not allow people to enter — great fear is there. Communist countries are very much afraid. If hippies start moving in Russia, communism will be gone — because then the Russian youth will see what is happening in other parts of the world : "People have become SO free, and we are prisoners!" They are not to be allowed to see that.

That's why people in Pune are against my sannyasins. What is the fear? If you are right and your religion is right and your morality is right, then why be afraid? The fear is that your morality is NOT right — it is repressive, it is forced, it is violent. And if your children see my free people, of course they would also like to be free. That is the fear. They would also like to hold the hand of some woman — which is NATURAL! graceful, lovely, divine. But Hindus are very much repressed — even to hold the hand of your own wife is a great revolution; even to talk to your own wife one feels guilty.

Now, these ugly hangovers of the past can be protected only if new fresh winds are not allowed to blow.

Sannyas is the beginning of a world citizenship. It is the beginning of a world which will be religious but without religions. Sannyas is not an idea, it is a device, it is a method — a method to uncondition you. And it is very good that children should be sannyasins from the very beginning — so nobody can condition them. Once they have tasted of freedom....

Neerja was telling me that little Siddartha falls in love with little girls — little Siddartha! — and not only that : sometimes he tries to make love to them. Now this is great! Now he has no inhibitions, no taboos. He will grow up into a beautiful human being.

To be a sannyasin means you will be allowing freedom to the children, you will not impose anything on them, you will not impose your ideas; you will NOT like them to become imitators. Sannyas is just symbolic of a great freedom!

WHY NOT LET THEM CHOOSE CONSCIOUSLY WHETHER AND WHEN TO TAKE SANNYAS?

In fact, many of them choose as consciously as you choose — many of them. When their parents become sannyasins, they are thrilled with the idea. Sometimes it happens just otherwise.

Geet Govind is here from Esalen : his daughter took sannyas first — just a small daughter! She has turned Esalen on — a small daughter, five or six years old. She became interested first in dynamic meditation and now it is difficult to prevent her — she goes on doing it, morning, evening; whenever she has time she does dynamic. Geet Govind was asking me how to stop her. And she enjoys it and she is going crazy in it. She became the catalytic agent... then the father, then the mother, then other people.

Life is so mysterious! One never knows from where the thing will start. And it is not the first case : many times it has happened that children have taken sannyas first, because they are of course more courageous. They don't CARE about others' opinions. They are not calculative. They are not worried about their jobs they have none. They are not worried about their wives or husbands — they have none. They are not worried about their children — they have none. They have no investment yet in life — they are free.

It happens many times : children take sannyas first, then the mother starts feeling, then the father starts feeling; then they also gather courage. So, many times children take the sannyas on their own. Sometimes the parents take first, then the children... they ARE interested. They also want to be orange people — what is it? — they want to be insiders! They don't want to be left outside.

And sometimes, only sometimes, very small children have been initiated — because their parents would like to protect them, to protect them from Christianity, to protect them from Mohammedanism, to protect them from Hinduism. I cannot say no because I know sannyas will be protective.

Sannyas gives NO ideology, but it protects you from other ideologies. Otherwise you cannot avoid it — your children will be conditioned. The church is after them, the politician is after them. You have to create some protection for your children, so that the priest and the politician don't come in; otherwise, they will grab hold of them — in the name of religious education, in the name of Sunday school, Bible class, this and that, they will catch hold of the child.

And once the child is conditioned, it becomes an unnecessary wastage of life and time and energy to uncondition him. It is better to leave him wild, leave him open.

And with sannyas, one thing is there : if your child when he is grown up wants to leave sannyas, nobody is there to prevent him. I am not preventing anybody from leaving! The moment you want to leave, you can leave without any guilt. That is for you!

If the child later on feels that he does not want to be a sannyasin, then who is after him? — he can leave it.

Sannyas is given easily and sannyas can be dropped as easily. There is no commitment as such. If there is any commitment, that is of your consciousness, that is your inner feeling — but nobody is after you, nobody will condemn you that "You have become a sinner and now you are bound for hell!"

The fifth question :

Today you told us to become responsible for our own lives and be responsive to our own inner being, and thus to take the reins back into our own hands from the hands of others. How does this fit in with surrendering the reins to you? I listen to my inner voice and sometimes it revolts against what you want me to do. Am I only hearing my ego? Are there any limits to surrendering to a master?

The question is from Swami Prem Pramod.

FIRST THING, PRAMOD, do you think you have surrendered to me? ever? for a single moment? My observation is that you have never surrendered. What do you want to take back? You have never surrendered! Those reins you have never surrendered — they are in your hands.

You were just befooling yourself that you had surrendered. What happens actually is : you ask me if you can do something with a decision already in the mind. If I say something which goes with your decision, you feel surrendered. You say, "Perfectly good how deeply I am surrendered to Osho!" If it does not go with your idea and your decision, then your inner voice says, "This is not right."

Surrender comes only when things go against your decision —

not when they go with your decision. Then what is the point of surrender?

And I have been watching Pramod : if things go HIS way, then he is absolutely surrendered. If even a slight thing goes against his idea, then the revolt....

Nobody is telling you to be in such a trouble. You can drop sannyas! Why create anguish unnecessarily for yourself? And I am interested now in helping many people to drop sannyas. Before the new commune, I want to sort my people. Either you are with me or you are not with me — both are good. Don't feel guilty! If you cannot surrender anything, at least you can surrender your sannyas to me — and that will be a great favour.

And you have some idea that you are obliging me by surrendering — what are you surrendering to me? I am not obliged to you. I am not gaining anything from your surrender, remember it perfectly well. What do you have to surrender to me? Your diseases, your madnesses, your ego, your mind, your past. I don't gain anything out of your egos or out of your illnesses and anxieties. So don't think that I am obliged to you, that you have done something great, a great favour to me by surrendering. Don't be stupid!

And when you surrender to me, do you think anything reaches to me? I am just an excuse. If you can surrender without any excuse, perfectly good. I am just a peg — you can hang your things on me, so that YOU are unburdened. That's the point. And once you have known the freedom of unburdening, once you have known the freedom that non-ego brings, then you will see the point : what surrender was. Then you will see that nothing was to be surrendered. You had nothing to surrender — just the idea of 'I', a very illusory idea, has been destroyed by surrender.

Surrender is like a thorn : you have a thorn in your foot; you have been walking in the garden and you have got a thorn in your foot — I supply you another thorn. This thorn can help the other thorn — you can take the other thorn out with it. When it is taken out, you have to throw both! because both are thorns.

Ego is a thorn, surrender is a thorn — it is just to take the ego out of you. It is a device. Once the ego is gone, SURRENDER IS GONE TOO! When the illness is gone, the medicine has no more relevance; you don't carry the bottle of it and the prescription of it. It is finished. But you will always be grateful, because without the other thorn you would have suffered from the first.

Surrender is a device to bring you out of your ego. If you DON'T want to come out of your ego, I am not much interested in bringing you out of your ego; it is none of my business. If YOU are interested, I am available. If YOU are not interested, perfectly good. The door is open....

And what inner voice can you have? The inner voice comes only when the ego has gone; otherwise, the ego goes on pretending to be your inner voice. The ego is a great pretender — beware of it.

And the last question :

Is the quality and expression of one's enlightenment richer, deeper and more creative if one allows oneself to complete one's worldly trips, rather than dropping them in the name of spirituality?

CERTAINLY! How can you drop if you have not lived your life totally? If you have not known sex, how can you drop it? It will linger, it will surround you in subtle ways; it will become an undercurrent in your unconscious. How can you drop anger if you have not lived it?

Nothing can be dropped without experiencing it in totality. Only total experience helps you to go beyond.

The spirituality that comes without experiencing life is impotent. That is the difference that I want to bring to your consciousness. That kind of spirituality has existed on the earth down the ages... and that's why man is so ugly. It is because of that kind of spirituality. It has made you repressed; it has not transformed you. It was against this, against that — against everything! It was against life, it was anti-life. It has not allowed you to live your life joyously — to see, to feel, to experience, and to go beyond through experiencing.

Knowledge liberates — not the knowledge that you gather from scriptures, but the knowledge that comes through experience. You become angry again and again and again... and you start feeling the foolishness of it, the utter ridiculousness of it, the poisonousness of it, the destructiveness of it. One day the fruit is ripe — not that you decide : "I will never be angry" — but just the fruit is ripe and it falls of its own accord. And anger disappears as if it had never existed in you; it simply evaporates.

Live your life. Live a life of variety, a multi-dimensional life, and you will be richer. And, naturally, when a man has lived in all the dimensions of his life and comes to enlightenment, his experience is going to be richer. At least his expression is going to be richer.

And finally : you can only come to enlightenment when you have lived truly. Those who think that they have come to enlightenment without living life are only deceiving themselves and nobody else. They are carrying the whole world in them — unlived, it remains there. Seeds they are carrying.

Patanjali divides samadhi, enlightenment, into two types : samadhi with seed and samadhi without seed. What he calls SABEEJ SAMADHI — samadhi with seed — is when you have not lived and subtle desires are still hankering to be fulfilled. You have repressed the seed but it is there, and it will assert itself when the right season arrives. When the spring comes, it may start sprouting again.

You can repress your sex for your whole life, but even at the moment of death it may assert itself.

Repression is not revolution. Revolution is through experience. Maturity is through experience. Enlightenment is ultimate maturity, beyond which there is none else. How can you find a shortcut to it? — there is none. You have to go through the whole life... tasting its sweetness and its bitterness, feeling its agonies and its ecstasies, watching its ups and downs, the sunlit peaks and the dark nights in the valley, the sadness and the joy of it — all has to be lived.

You have to be a sinner and a saint! One who is only a saint is a poor saint, and one who is only a sinner is a poor sinner — you have to be saintsinner or sinnersaint. You have to live ALL that God makes available to you. You have to live it unconditionally. And then one day... the quantum leap, the enlightenment.

A beautiful story for you to meditate :

Pope Paul XV lay in the Vatican close to death. Scores of doctors were consulted, but none could come up with an answer. A pall of anxiousness hung in the air. All the possibilities were cancelled out. Finally one doctor came and said that the Pope's state was due to his life-long celibacy and the only thing to do was for him to make love — once would be enough.

A very embarrassed bishop came to break the awful news. "Your-a Holiness-a," he began, "You hafta maka da love to a woman-a to save-a your life-a. Terrible-a news-a I have-a to geeve-a you."

The Pope looked up slowly. "Dees is a sad-a, sad-a day-a for da Catholic-a church-a; there's-a no-a other-a way-a?"

The bishop shook his head. "No-a, Your-a Holiness-a, I'm afraid-a not-a!"

"Well-a," said the Pope. "Eef I-a must-a, den I-a must-a do-a dees-a terrible-a thing-a. But I do eet on-a four-a condeetions-a only-a."

"Yes, yes-a, anything-a," said the bishop, somewhat relieved. "And what-a are your-a four condeetions-a?"

The Pope drew a long breath.

"First-a, she must-a be a Catholic-a."

"Of course-a, Your Holiness-a."

"Second-a, she-a must-a be a virgin-a."

"Yes, Your Holiness-a."

"Third-a, she must-a wear-a a blind-a fold-a so-a she-a does-a not see-a who ees-a doing dees thing-a to her-a."

"Yes-a, Your Holiness-a, and-a da fourth-a?"

"Fourth-a, fourth-a, she gotta have da beeg-a tits-a and da nice-a bum-bum!"

CHAPTER
5

Playfulness Is Heaven

The first question :

I live in the land of seriousness, imprisoned in its borders. Can you draw me a road-map to your land of leela? Have I a defective gene? I cannot find my laughter or light-heartedness. I see it around me, but do not feel it in me.

$\mathscr{S}$ARJANA, THERE CANNOT BE ANY MAP TO THE LAND OF PLAYFULNESS. All maps lead to seriousness. Playfulness is when all maps have been burnt down. There is no way to playfulness, because playfulness is not a goal and cannot be a goal. When you forget about goals, when you are not going anywhere, when the very idea of going is dropped, then herenow playfulness starts growing in you, happening in you.

Playfulness is not then and there : it is herenow. So how can there be a road-map? You are not to go : you are just to be.

Seriousness is goal-oriented. And even when a serious person starts playing, he transforms the quality of the play — it becomes a game; it is no more play. That is the difference between a game and a play. When a play becomes serious, it becomes a game.

People go to see wrestling, people go to see bullfights or American football — ugly, violent, inhuman. The people who are going to see these things are immature, a little perverted too. The spectators are as ungrown as the gladiators. And both are in some way catharting; in the name of the game, they are throwing their rubbish, they are simply vomiting their violence.

This is a very violent, violent world! That's why love cannot exist here. When human beings will really be human beings, things like bullfighting and wrestling will be unheard of, they will become part of history. Just to imagine that thousands of people have come to see a bullfight looks so ugly, disgusting. But people are serious. They change the play also into seriousness.

A play is something in which a goal is not at all concerned. The very being together is beautiful! for the sheer joy of it! In a better world, with more understanding, games will disappear — there will only be plays. There will be nobody as a winner, nobody as the defeated — because the very idea of defeating and winning is inhuman. There is no NEED for it! Why can't we enjoy the sheer togetherness? There should be no counting, no marking. There should not be any result out of it.

If you are in love with playing football, play football! Just play it! Don't look for the result. If the result comes in, you become serious, the play is destroyed; it has become almost businesslike. Enjoy the sheer outpour of energy. Enjoy the moment — don't sacrifice it for anything else.

That's what LEELA is, playfulness is. But you are in love and it becomes serious, and you start thinking of marriage and you start thinking of having children and you start thinking of having a family — and the whole thing has gone ugly! If these things happen, let them happen as by-products, not as results. Yes, if you love a woman, you would like to be with her — this is marriage! There should be no other marriage. There should not even be the idea, because the VERY idea makes things down-to-earth; the poetry is destroyed. It becomes mundane; the romance is destroyed.

But the moment you are in love, immediately your mind starts weaving and spinning... about family, how to have a family of one's own. Why should you need 'a family of one's own'? People possess things and people possess people too. If you possess things, it can be forgiven, but how can it be forgiven when you start possessing people? You say 'my wife', 'my husband', 'my child' — what have you DONE to call this child yours? Who are you? How do you come in? Can you create a child? Can you create the child according to your own desire?

A child comes from the unknown, is a gift. You are not the creator, how can you be the possessor? It is NOT according to you that the child takes shape and form and being.

You were longing for a beautiful child and you are hit with a lulu and still you call it 'my child' You have been just a passage in the great play of existence.

Just as there are liberation movements, women's lib movement, so a new movement should be mounted : children's liberation movement. Nobody should be allowed to possess children. Possessiveness should not be allowed! Nobody should say 'my child'. All children are of God. You can only be a caretaker, not more than that. And you should be grateful that you have been chosen to be a caretaker of a new life evolving. That is more than enough! Enjoy the game of it! of being a caretaker of an evolving life, but don't start possessing.

But our mind is possessive. The possessiveness has gone to the very roots, and that has been the greatest hindrance in human growth.

When love is possessive it becomes exclusive. Then 'this woman is mine, and exclusively mine!' — then she cannot laugh with anybody else, then she cannot hold hands with anybody else, then she cannot look into the eyes of somebody else. What nonsense! Why? Who am I to possess? And how can love be possessive?

Love is always inclusive; it can never be exclusive. If I love the woman, I will love to see her happy in a thousand and one ways, with a thousand and one people. I would like her to be happy. That will be my joy. If she is happy dancing with somebody, I should not feel jealous — I love her! how can I feel jealous? I should be thrilled that she is happy. But when you claim that she is YOUR wife, then you cannot allow this. You start crippling her. She starts paralyzing you in revenge. You both become destructive to each other.

Love is the greatest creative energy, but up to now it has been a misfortune, the greatest misfortune. People have not been killed because of hatred : people have been killed because of love. Life has become so bitter, not because of anger : it has become so bitter because of love.

You fight for the love of a woman or a man; you fight for the love of your family or clan. You fight for the love of your ideology or religion; you fight for the love of your mother-country or father-country, fatherland, motherland. You go on fighting for your love! All murders, all killings — all kinds of sufferings exist because of your so-called love.

Something is basically wrong with your love — your love is a fixated love; it is not a flowing play. It is serious, it is exclusive, it is possessive. It is full of stupidity.

One should be able to see all this — and just SEEING it, you start relaxing. You see the point of it and you start relaxing, and a new awareness arises in you.

Just.... I am surprised when I come across a man whose wife has died — and he is still crying and in anguish : his beloved has died. Why be so monopolistic? There are so many beautiful women still alive! This makes no sense. Your husband has died and for your whole life you will remain in a nightmare — because you cannot love anybody else? Your love is so tiny? so fixated? it was a kind of obsession? It was neurotic, it was not healthy. Otherwise, when the husband is dead, yes, there will be sadness, but you will say goodbye and you will move. You will not sacrifice your life — because sacrificing your life is dangerous. If you sacrifice your life and you become a martyr, you will take revenge on life; you will create guilt in your children, you will create guilt all around. And you WILL suffer! And when a person suffers, he creates vibes of suffering all around.

No, this makes no sense! The world is full of so many people, why should you be so fixated? But the fixation comes from the very beginning : the moment a child says 'my mother', and the mother feels very happy, the fixation has started. Now the child will remain obsessed his whole life.

And when the child is small, he is naturally dependent on the mother — and mothers and fathers have exploited that dependence immensely. He is helpless, he cannot survive on his or her own; he HAS to look up to the mother and the father.

His helplessness is exploited. He knows if the mother is gone, he will be dead. If the mother is no more available, he will be dead, he will not be able to survive. This idea goes on and on getting deeper and deeper.... And the mother helps it, because the mother enjoys the ego trip that "You cannot survive without me." She threatens many times, "Listen to me, otherwise I will leave and go forever, or I will die — and THEN you will know!" And the child is shaken to the very roots — he cannot survive without the mother.

This becomes, by and by, a conditioning. Later on it will be reflected in all his relationships. He will think the same about his wife : if the wife is no more, he will not be able to survive. This will become unconscious. He will think the same again and again about everything : "If this job is gone, then I am finished. If this house is no more with me, then where will I be? If this bank balance is no more with me, then where will I be?" His whole life he will think in terms of fixation, and his whole life will be a long long, unnecessary suffering. He is no more a child, but he remains childish because of the conditioning.

Love, and immediately you turn it into bitterness because you become serious about it. You start thinking of the future. Think of the future — marriage, children, security — and you have destroyed the play and it has become a game, and a very dangerous game. And you will be a loser — nobody is ever a winner.

With play, everybody is a winner. With seriousness, nobody is ever a winner — all are losers.

You come to meditate here and you become serious about it. And I go on insisting : Don't become serious. Meditation can happen only in playfulness, in utter playfulness, when you are not searching and seeking for anything, when you are simply dancing or singing or chanting; when you are not asking, when the activity is all and all in itself, no future is provoked, no future is involved in it... then it happens. Meditation is a happening.

You cannot snatch it from God's hands. You cannot desire it and you cannot have it. You can only do one thing : you can become an empty receiving end — and that's what happens when you are playful.

Meditation is fun! Even the word looks absurd with meditation — meditation and fun? Down the ages, you have been taught that this is the seriousmost thing : go into the church and become serious — even if you don't have one, create a long face, then you will look as if you are in the church. Don't laugh, don't dance, don't be playful! — it is a serious affair. You are facing God.

This God seems to be somehow very strange! He cannot allow laughter, He cannot allow dance, He cannot allow love, He cannot allow joy. The Gods of the past were very revengeful, jealous Gods, violent Gods; ready to crush you and destroy you, ready to throw you into hell-fire. Even the idea of God was ugly.

Here with me, you will have to learn a new language : meditation is fun, prayer is love and laughter; and the temple, the church, the mosque, is the place to enjoy, the place to be drunk with life; the place to dance and hold hands, the place to share what God has given to you, the place to be absorbed utterly into the moment. That is the meaning of fun, that is the meaning of laughter, that is the meaning of joy : to be utterly absorbed in the moment as if no other moment exists. So how can you ask for a result? Result needs another moment in the future.

Become like small children — dancing, singing, shouting — and God will come to you unawares. Suddenly one moment, you will find He is surrounding you; suddenly you will find you are not holding the hands of a woman — God is holding your hands; you are not holding the hands of a man — it is God. Looking into the eyes of the other, playfully, joyously, suddenly you will fall into a depth unknown to you, unknown to your mind. You will start disappearing into a deep abyss.

That's what God is! God is not in the scriptures — it is in the eyes of people, and in the flowers and in the rivers and in the moons. God is written all over the place! Don't go 'to the scriptures. And if you cannot find God in alive trees, green and red and gold, if you cannot find God there, you will not find Him in the Bible, the Koran and the Vedas. How can you find Him there if you cannot find Him here? Once you have found it here, you will find it anywhere... then He is everywhere.

Once found, God is everywhere — but you will have to find Him in life, in playfulness.

Playfulness makes you alive to the maximum. Seriousness cripples you. You become shrunken, frozen. You become closed, you become isolated. You become egoistic. That's why seriousness has been so much cherished by people because seriousness gives you the ego, and playfulness takes the ego away.

You ask me, Sarjana : I LIVE IN THE LAND OF SERIOUSNESS, IMPRISONED IN ITS BORDERS.

You can exist only in the land of seriousness — you as an 'I'; and you can exist only imprisoned in the borders of seriousness — as an 'I'. If you want to be playful, you will have to drop the idea of 'I'. The 'I' cannot be playful; it resists play, because play is death to it. The 'I' is always serious.

Have you not watched it? When you laugh, just have a look inside : the 'I' disappears. That's why egoistic people cannot laugh — impossible! When you are dancing, a moment comes when the 'I' disappears. But egoistic people cannot dance; they cannot allow the 'I' to disappear ever. Naturally, they will remain imprisoned, they will be prisoners. But this is your choice!

If you want the ego, you will have to accept the prison, you will have to accept the boundaries. If you want a bigger and still bigger ego, the prison will become smaller and smaller, and the walls of the prison will come closer and closer. If you want to become the greatest ego in the world, you will be nothing but a prison, you will be surrounded by China Walls from everywhere, you will live in a straitjacket, behind iron walls.

But if you want to be alive, then the ego has to be dropped. Ego is a distraction from life.

I LIVE, you say, IN THE LAND OF SERIOUSNESS, IMPRISONED IN ITS BORDERS. CAN YOU DRAW ME A ROAD-MAP TO YOUR LAND OF LEELA?

And you are again asking about a road-map — that is a serious thing. I have none. If you want road-maps you will have to go to the churches and to the priests — they have. Actually! — in Indian temples there are maps of heaven, hell, and how to reach there, and what you will find... the whole geography! Who is who, and where God lives, and where the great saints live — everything you will find.

They have charted all the maps — all imaginary! because God cannot be caught in any map. And heaven is not a map, neither is hell; they are not geographical at all — they are psychological states. When you are serious, you are in hell; seriousness is hell, playfulness is heaven.

You ask me : CAN YOU DRAW ME A ROAD-MAP TO YOUR LAND OF LEELA? HAVE I A DEFECTIVE GENE?

No — nobody has a defective gene. And a defective gene does not create the problem : the problem comes from the ego. And the ego has nothing to do with the body; the ego is a mind attitude.

You have a mind and that is your defect. I will not say that you have a defective mind — mind is the defect. You will have to drop the mind. And dropping it, suddenly you will find you have always been in the land of leela; not for a single moment had you left it — nobody can leave it. We can just forget about it. We can become serious and we can forget about it.

You are still the children playing on the sea beach. You are still the children searching for seashells on the beach. You are still the children collecting wild flowers. You are still the children trying to catch hold of a butterfly. That purity of childhood is still there; it has not been taken away from you — it has only been superimposed by seriousness, ego, mind. It is there! The rock is blocking the fountain, but the fountain has not disappeared. Remove the rock and the fountain flows again in all its splendour.

You say : I CANNOT FIND MY LAUGHTER OR LIGHT-HEARTEDNESS.

Seeking, you will never find it. Finding, or the effort to find it, is a serious thing. IT IS HERE! — you need not find it. Start enjoying it! Start being cheerful this very moment! Don't try to find it, because if you try to find it you will remain serious. How can a seeker be non-serious?

You are searching for happiness and laughter and joy —you have to be serious, otherwise how will you search? Meanwhile you will remain serious, and the seriousness is getting stronger every moment. Tomorrow again you will search; but one day has passed — twenty-four hours' more conditioning of seriousness is on you. You will find less laughter tomorrow; the day after tomorrow it will become even more difficult... and so on and so forth. And you will always be searching and seeking and trying to find.

Just be cheerful THIS moment! Just see the point of it! Don't postpone it — these are tricks of postponing, Sarjana. You don't WANT to be happy; you still want to remain unhappy. You still want some new excuse to be unhappy. Now this is the excuse : "I am searching for happiness, I am searching for joy. Right now I am unhappy. I will be happy when I have found — but how can I be happy right now? I will have to find, and the journey is long and the path is arduous, an uphill task." So you can be happy with your unhappiness right now, and tomorrow we will see... and tomorrow never comes.

Don't try to postpone — these are tricks the mind goes on playing upon you. Be happy! Have a good laugh! Have a good dance!

In the beginning it may look a little awkward, because you have not laughed for so long. The lips may have lost their elasticity. But it will come... just give a little opportunity for the lips to learn it again. They cannot lose it. Maybe forgotten — it will be revived again.

One can never forget how to laugh. It is like swimming : you cannot forget it. Once you have known it, you cannot forget. You may not go to the river for fifty years; after fifty years, suddenly, you can swim. You will not even need to remember it.

And you have been laughing when you were a child. Every child is born laughing, and there are very very few fortunate people who die laughing. One who can die laughing has arrived. But if you want to die laughing, you will have to live laughing.

Once an old Parsi came to see me and he said, "Do you know? We have a beautiful story about Zarathustra — that he was born laughing."

I said, "That is nothing special — every child is born laughing."

Zarathustra is simply a symbol. Every child is born alive, full of joy! great energy, great love for life, great curiosity, infinite wonder, awe for small things. Every child is born an adventurer, an explorer. And every child is born with great courage to go into the unknown. We cripple him. We stop him. We prevent him. We start cultivating — and whatsoever we call cultivation is nothing but destroying all the possibilities, allowing only small holes for him to live in, taking his whole sky away and giving him a very small corner in the world.

He was born as all men, all women, all animals, all trees, all rivers, all mountains are. And what do we do with the child? We take all that he has brought away from him; we make him a doctor, an engineer, a businessman, a soldier, a politician — we confine him. He was born as all, as infinity; all the alternatives were open. We close all the alternatives and leave only one alternative open. We have killed him! We allow only a minute part of him to live.

Just think of a businessman : he simply lives as a businessman. Morning, afternoon, evening, night, he lives as a businessman. He dreams of business, he talks of business, he reads of business — his whole life has become business. What have you done to this man? What misfortune has happened to this man? He cannot be anything else! He does not know how to relax. He does not know how to slip out of this small hole in which he has started living — he calls it businessman, doctor, engineer, professor.

A man should be liquid; he should be able to be all. You should not live only as you — you should live as all humanity, past, future, present. You should live as a totality; multidimensional you should live, not one-dimensional, not linear. To live like a line is to live a very poor life.

There is no need! But we have all become focussed in small corners, tethered in small corners we call our minds, egos, this and that. And we are so much obsessed with those small places, caves — dirty and dark, dismal and sad. But we have become accustomed to those places and we are afraid of the open air and we are afraid of the open sky and the sun and the sand, and we never go out of those small spaces. Hence, laughter has disappeared.

Life has disappeared! — how can laughter live without life? Your spirit is dead. And this is a miracle, that your so-called spiritual people are the MOST spiritless people —and you call them spiritual. My definition of the word 'spiritual' is : one who is spirited, one who lives a passionate life, with intensity; who lives at the maximum, not at the minimum; who does not live a lukewarm life.

Be courageous! and laughter will follow. Be courageous and live intensely! and you will not need to ask how to be playful. Out of the maximum, playfulness happens of its own accord — because when you live at the maximum you start overflowing. That overflowing of energies is what playfulness is — there is no map to it, there is no technique to it. Just understanding.

The second question :

The human civilization is collapsing all around the world. What do you have to say about it?

REJOICE IN ITS COLLAPSE!

The third question :

Why is it that 'going with the flow' makes me feel guilty? Please talk about guilt.

It is the guilt factor that makes floating so unattractive.

PADMA, GUILT IS ONE OF THE GREATEST PROBLEMS everybody has to encounter. The whole past of humanity has been guilt-ridden. And each generation goes on giving its diseases to the new generation. And they go on becoming more and more. Naturally. They accumulate with each generation. And each new generation is more burdened than the previous one.

But guilt has been one of the basic strategies of the priests to exploit people. The priest cannot exist without guilt. When you feel guilty, remember, the priest is around you. When you feel guilty, remember, the priest's hands are around your neck — he is killing you. Guilt is a strategy to exploit people, to turn people into slaves.

Try to understand the mechanism of it. Only that understanding will help you to get out of it. What exactly is guilt?

First : it is a condemnation of life; it is a life-negative attitude. You have been told something is basically wrong with life; you have been told that you are born a sinner. You have been told that nothing good can come out of life or out of you or out of anybody else. Nothing good is possible on this earth! Good is with God. And you have to find a saviour — a Christ, a Krishna — you have to find a saviour who can save you from yourselves, who can take you to God.

Life is not worth living — avoid living! If you live, you will get deeper and deeper into sin — life is sin. Avoid life. Withdraw yourself from life. And whenever you feel you are attracted towards life, guilt arises. You start feeling you are going to do something wrong.

And life is immensely beautiful. It has great attraction, gravitation to it. It is natural to be attracted by life. It is natural to be in love. It is natural to enjoy, it is natural to laugh, it is natural to dance. But ALL that is natural has been condemned. You have to go against nature — that has been the teaching down the ages.

The puritans have poisoned your natural sources of life; they have made you against yourself! They have created a split in you. They could not corrupt the body, but they have corrupted the mind. So the mind exists according to the priests, and the body exists according to nature — and there is no meeting.

The body desires the joys of life — all joys. The body is life-affirmative and the mind is life-negative. The mind represents the priests — Christian, Hindu, Jain. The mind goes on talking in the language of the priests; it goes on saying "This is wrong!" If you are eating food and you enjoy the taste, Mahatma Gandhi speaks from your mind : "This is wrong — don't enjoy the taste. To enjoy taste is sin."

In Mahatma Gandhi's ashram one of the basic disciplines was ASWAD — no taste. You have to eat just to fulfill bodily needs, but you should not take any taste, you should not enjoy the flavour of the food, the smell of the food. You should destroy the food so it doesn't taste, and you should destroy your tongue too so it loses sensitivity to taste. When you lose taste, you have become a mahatma.

The same has been true about other things : if you fall in love with a woman, you are falling in sin, something wrong is happening. If you see the beautiful face of a woman or a man, and you are thrilled, fascinated, great guilt arises — what are you doing? This is irreligious!

And if you are a married man, then more so. You have a wife, you have committed yourself to her. Now, even to appreciate the beauty of another woman is impossible. You will go home feeling guilty. You have not done anything! You had just seen a beautiful woman pass by. Now, this is an ugly state of affairs. You will feel guilty; you will feel defensive. When you go back home you will try to hide yourself. You will not allow your wife to know that on the road you saw a beautiful woman and it was a great joy to see her — because if you say that, there will be trouble. And why create trouble? You will lie. And when you lie you will feel guilty again because you are lying, and one should not lie to one's own wife. Now, so on and so forth.... One guilt creates another, and so on and so forth, ad nauseam. It goes on and on. There is no end to it. Then you become guilt-ridden; you carry a Himalaya of guilt on your heart.

And EACH thing has been condemned.

You will not get rid of the guilt unless you understand the whole mechanism of it — how it is through guilt that the priest has dominated humanity, how the priest has created a slavery, and a subtle slavery. You don't have chains on your hands, you don't have chains on your feet, but you have chains deep inside your soul.

To be free of guilt is to be free of all priesthood. To be free of guilt is to be free of all past. And to be free of guilt is to become one, because then the split disappears. To be free of guilt is to drop schizophrenia. And then there is great joy, because you are no longer fighting with yourself. You start living!

How can you live if you are continuously fighting? You cannot live if you go on fighting with yourself. You can live only when the fight has been dropped. Then life has its own rhythm, its own melody. And life is such a blessing. And only in that harmony, when you are one, with NO guilt, with NO repression, with NO taboos, with NO inhibitions, with NO priest interfering in your life — Hindu, Mohammedan, Christian — when you are on your own, uninterfered with, your own master, then only can you contact God.

The priest has made it impossible! If you cannot contact life, how can you contact life abundant? If you cannot contact flowers, how can you contact the one who has created them? If you cannot contact beauty, joy, love, how can you contact the one from where all beauty, love and joy comes, flows? Impossible. The priest has made it impossible.

The priest is the cause why the earth has become irreligious. Without destroying priesthoods and the old churches and old religions, the world will remain irreligious.

I teach you a new religion! Not Christianity, not Hinduism, not Jainism, not Buddhism. I teach you a new kind of religiousness — guilt-free, tabooless, non-repressive. I teach you a religion of joy, acceptance, naturalness, spontaneity.

Padma, you ask : WHY IS IT THAT 'GOING WITH THE FLOW' MAKES ME FEEL GUILTY?

BECAUSE GOING WITH THE FLOW MAKES YOU FEEL HAPPY — that's why. And you cannot allow happiness. Happiness has become associated with guilt. Go back, Padma, to your childhood — you will find causes there. Just remember, go backwards; try to find out when it happened.

A small child knows nothing of guilt; he is wild and primitive. That's why to see a small child is such a joy. He is as yet uncrippled, he is as yet uncivilized. He has not been introduced to the disease called civilization — that's why he has so much energy, so much flow. The child is streaming, vibrating; he is a great dynamo; he is all dance. He cannot contain himself — he has so much that he is overflowing. You cannot make a child sit silently. Why? Because the energy is so much, uncontainable.

The child wants to enjoy everything, and the parents are guilt-ridden. The child wants to shout and he enjoys shouting; that is his expression, that is his creativity. That shout, if helped and not destroyed, will become his song — that is the beginning of the song. But we stop him. We say, "Don't shout! This is ugly, this is bad, this is unmannerly. This is not done in the society. You belong to a famous family, you belong to a great, respectable family — you should not do this. This is okay for the urchins, but not for you. You represent us : look how serious we are. We never shout — and you are shouting?"

And the child was enjoying the shouting so much. In fact, when you stop him shouting you have condemned his joy — that's what he will understand deep down, existentially. What will happen to him? He cannot understand why shouting is wrong; he has as yet no mind to understand that kind of rubbishness. He was enjoying — that he understands; that shouting brings such joy, such flow. He feels so high, he feels so turned on. Just by shouting, his energy starts moving, he becomes a riverlike flow, he becomes a roaring phenomenon, a tidal wave.

Now you say, "Don't shout — this is bad." What are you saying actually? How will the child translate it? The child will think, "My joy is not accepted."

The child does not want to go to sleep; he is feeling so alive and you force him and you drag him to the bed. He is trying to get away from you and he is saying, "I am NOT feeling like sleep. I DON'T want to go to sleep. I want to play a little more!" But you don't listen. You say, "It is time and you have to go to sleep."

Now what are you doing to the child? You are rejecting — you are rejecting his instinctive understandings. He does not feel like going to sleep right now — how can he be made to sleep? There is no way! You can force him; he will lie there underneath the blanket and will weep and cry and will feel rejected, will feel unaccepted by the family, will feel guilty about why he cannot go to sleep when the mother wants him to. Now, what can he do? The sleep is not coming. And in the morning when he is feeling sleepy, you drag him out and you say, "Get out! It is time to get up." And he wants to sleep a little more.

Now you interfere — wherever he feels joy, you interfere. Naturally, you make him feel again and again that his joy is wrong.

That gets deep into your bloodstream. That's what has happened to you, Padma. So whenever you are going with the flow it means something is wrong. You are feeling happy? you immediately hear your mother's voice : "Padma, what are you doing? Feeling happy? Betraying me? Betraying your dad, betraying your family? Look how serious we are — and is it good to betray your mother? Look at what long faces we have — and what are you doing? flowing with the flow? going with the flow? Never has it happened in our family! And it should not happen."

You start feeling guilty. Just watch when you start feeling guilty, listen silently... you will find your parental voices, your mother, your father, your teacher, saying, "This is not right."

While you make love to a man, you will feel guilty, because your mother has told you that this is wrong, this is the greatest sin. When you start making love to a man, something in you feels it is not right — the mother is standing there, the father is standing there, and it looks so embarrassing with the parents standing... and you are making love to a man?! What are you doing? Stop it! You may not stop, but you will not go totally into it — which is far worse than stopping. It is better to stop! You cannot stop either, because then your whole nature feels discontented. And you cannot go totally in it because your mind says this is wrong. So you go half-heartedly, half way, and you exist in a limbo. You never go to the totality of it — SO YOU NEVER FEEL SATISFIED. Out of it you only gather more frustration; you again find you have failed once more, that's all. It has not happened this time again.

And you start wondering whether this orgasm is just an invention, whether some masochistic people have invented it, or some sadistic people have invented it, just to make people feel tortured — because it is not happening to me!

You will be surprised: this is the first century after at least five thousand years that a few women are feeling orgasm. For five thousand years, women have NOT felt orgasm. That too is happening only in the Western hemisphere. I have not come across a single Indian woman who feels orgasm — she has not even heard about the word. In Indian languages we don't have any word for orgasm — because the thing has not existed so the word was never needed. Even in the West, only ten, twelve percent of women are feeling orgasm. This is ugly!

And what to say about men? Do you think men feel orgasm? Ejaculation is not orgasm. Orgasm is a very very different phenomenon. So man can deceive himself easily because he can feel ejaculation, so he thinks he has orgasm — that is not so. Ejaculation is a very local phenomenon, just the triggering of a physical mechanism — a release, a relief, nothing more.

Orgasm is ecstasy. Orgasm is getting lost into timelessness. Orgasm is when your whole body vibrates with some unknown energy that you have never come across. Orgasm is when you are very close to God.

The word orgasm comes from *orgia* — it was a religious ceremony, a pagan ceremony, when people became ecstatic, so ecstatic, that their whole body was full of divine energy, and they were bursting with energy, and they were lost in that energy — that was called *orgia*. It was a religious pagan ceremony; it was something like Tantra. It was Dionysian. The word 'orgasm' comes from that ceremony.

Men also rarely feel it. When your whole body throbs, not only your sexual organ but your whole body throbs, from toe to head you become a sexual orgasm, you become a sexual organ.... That is the symbol of Shiva; you must have seen in India the Shiva-linga. You may sometimes be wondering, "Where are the eyes and where is the nose and where is the mouth and where are the legs? and what kind of image is this?"

This is the symbol of orgasm: when the whole body turns into a sexual organ. From eyes, mouth, body, mind — all disappear into sexuality, into sensuality, into a kind of immense sensitivity. That is the meaning of Shiva-linga.

Orgasm has become impossible because you cannot go totally with the flow. And with orgasm becoming impossible, a thousand and one diseases have become prevalent in man. Wilhelm Reich is right that if we can bring orgasm back to humanity, almost ninety percent of mental diseases will IMMEDIATELY disappear — like dewdrops in the morning when the sun comes.

Ninety percent of mental diseases exist because man has forgotten how to be rejuvenated with God, how to fall into divine energy, and come back again resurrected. Those blocked energies are creating problems. But now... first the priest created the guilt, now the psychoanalyst is against Wilhelm Reich — because, the psychoanalyst, where will he go if ninety percent of mental diseases disappear? If Reich is right, then what about the Freudians and the Adlerians and the Jungians and others — what will happen to them? Reich was condemned as mad, was forced into imprisonment — and he was one of the greatest geniuses of this age, who had a real insight. But this is what we always do : we crucify! He died condemned as a madman in a prison.

Man has not changed much. Two thousand years have passed, but we go on doing the same as we did with Jesus. Now, this man was releasing a very very significant truth — that man's mental illnesses will continue and will go on becoming bigger and bigger, and soon it will be impossible to treat man. Out of four, three persons are already abnormal, and the fourth is just on the way, any moment.... This is not a good situation!

Reich is right that something has to be done. First the priest was involved, now the modern priest is the psychoanalyst. First the priest had the investment in making people feel guilty; he created guilt. Because of guilt, he stopped people's being orgasmic. And now the psychoanalyst is enjoying the results — his profession is flourishing like anything. His is the most needed profession, and the most respected.

Physicians are no more needed as much as the psychoanalyst is needed, because the body is getting better and better every day and mind is getting worse and worse every day.

Guilt has created human pathology.

In the future, the priest is not needed, neither is the psychoanalyst needed. Both those professions are anti-human; they should go. But they can go only if man is freed of guilt, otherwise they cannot go.

So, Padma, even if you feel guilty, go with the flow. Ignore the guilt. Let the guilt be there; in spite of it, go with the flow! The more you go with the flow, the more you will become able to catch yourself and avoid getting caught into the trap of guilt — you will be able to catch yourself in time. You will be able to slip out of that guilt prison.

One has to get out of it, otherwise life will be a long, sad, meaningless anguish.

The fourth question :

Osho, if one were to make only one new year's resolution, what would you suggest?

ANURAG, THIS AND ONLY THIS CAN BE THE NEW YEAR'S RESOLUTION : I resolve never to make any resolutions because all resolutions are restrictions for the future. All resolutions are imprisonments. You decide today for tomorrow? You have destroyed tomorrow.

Allow the tomorrow to have its own being. Let it COME in its own way! Let it bring its own gifts.

Resolution means you will allow only this and you will not allow that. Resolution means you would like the sun to rise in the west and not in the east. If it rises in the east, you will not open your windows; you will keep your windows open to the west.

What is resolution? Resolution is struggle. Resolution is ego. Resolution is saying, "I cannot live spontaneously." And if you cannot live spontaneously, you don't live at all — you only pretend.

So let only one resolution be there : I will never make any resolutions. Drop all resolutions! Let life be a natural spontaneity. The only golden rule is that there are no golden rules.

CHAPTER

6

Think Without Mind

The first question :

Osho, you say we cannot take full responsibility for ourselves until we are 'awakened'. The Western growth movement says we cannot be awakened until we take full responsibility for ourselves. Is there a conflict? Please comment.

ANAND SALAM, THERE IS NO CONFLICT AT ALL — it is just seeing the same phenomenon from two different angles. They are two aspects of the same event; they are together, they are simultaneous. There is no contrariness in them : they are complementary.

When I say you can take full responsibility for yourselves only when you are awakened, I mean that you don't even know who you are — how can you take responsibility for something you are not even aware of? You are acquainted only with the tip of the iceberg — how can you take responsibility for the unconscious, which is nine times more than the conscious? The conscious, at the most, can take responsibility for the conscious. Even that is difficult because it is constantly influenced by the unconscious. You are pulled, dragged into things by the unconscious — you don't know why.

You fall in love with a man or a woman — how can you take responsibility for it? because falling in love is not a conscious decision on your part. It is an unconscious phenomenon. It simply overwhelms you; suddenly one day, you find that you are in love. You have not done anything for it, you have not prepared for it, you were not planning for it. It comes out of nowhere, out of the blue... and you are possessed by it, you are madly possessed by it. How can you take responsibility for your love? Love comes from roots about which you are not aware.

That's why I say unless you are awakened you will not be able to take total responsibility. Your responsibility will be fragmentary, superficial, shallow.

And the growth movement people are also true : they say we cannot be awakened until we take full responsibility for ourselves. Yes, how will you be awakened? You have to start taking responsibility. It cannot be total right now —let it be partial. It cannot be absolute right now — let it not be absolute. It can only be fragmentary; it cannot be total. No need to worry. Even a fragmentary responsibility is far better than irresponsibility. Even to be aware about a small part of your being is far better than not to be aware.

The choice is not between total awareness and partial awareness : the choice before you is between partial awareness and NO awareness. Choose partial awareness; that's what the growth people say — they are true. And when you choose to be responsible for a few things, you will become a little more alert. When you become a little more alert, you will be able to become a little more responsible... and so on and so forth.

The more responsible you become, the more alert; the more alert you become, the more responsible. They will go hand in hand.

The growth movement is a gradual process of enlightenment. What I am saying is not a process but a metanoia, a metamorphosis, a transformation, a sudden transformation. If you understand me, in a single moment, like lightning, you can become enlightened. But if you don't understand me, then you will have to crawl slowly through group methods, meditations, prayers, Yoga, Tantra, Tao... you will have to move slowly, slowly. Either you become enlightened instantly, this moment, or you have to grow into it slowly, slowly. The growth movement is a movement for growth; growth can only be gradual.

What I am teaching to you is sudden enlightenment. It needs NO time; not even a single moment is needed. Listen to me! and in this very moment... because what I am saying or what I am trying to say is that you ARE already enlightened. You need not be enlightened. You have simply forgotten; it is a kind of forgetfulness. Not that you have to become — you ARE that. Just a recognition, just a turning in, just a deep look inside yourself...

and you will start laughing. You have always been there! You had never left in the first place.

Enlightenment is your nature.

But there are two types of people and you cannot clo anything about your type. Either like a Hui Neng, listening to the four lines of the Diamond Sutra, you become enlightened. Now, you cannot ask how to become Hui Neng; that is not possible. Either you are or you are not; there is no more to it.

Hearing about Hui Neng, down the centuries, many people have been cramming the Diamond Sutra, particularly those four lines. Day in, day out, people have been repeating them. "If Hui Neng can become enlightened just by hearing four lines of the Diamond Sutra, then why can't I?" But you go on repeating — the more you repeat, the more unenlightened you will be. It can't happen that way! You are not a Hui Neng; things are finished there.

With sudden enlightenment that is the problem : either it happens or it doesn't happen. You cannot do anything about it. It is beyond you. The BHAKTAS have called it the grace of God — as if it comes from Him, it is a gift; you need not be worthy of it. Only one person in thousands, or even in millions, is capable of that. All the remaining ones have to move slowly, have to move gradually.

That's why here I go on talking about instant enlightenment, and I go on sending you into groups, meditations, processes. Sometimes people come to me and ask, "If enlightenment is possible right now then why do you send us? Why do you make us suffer — in the Primal, in the Encounter, in the Gestalt? Why do you send us to these Rolfers who are very skillful torturers?" What can I do? If you cannot listen to me, you will have to go to the Rolfers. Either you become awakened right now — it is your choice — or go on... then I will send you to the groups. They will torture you, goad you, provoke you, pull you this way and that. They will create such misery for you that you will decide finally that it is better to become enlightened rather than suffer so much.

And unless you say to me "Now I am enlightened" I will go on sending you. They help.

You have to follow the long, the hard way, if you cannot understand the shortcut, if you cannot take the jump, then you will have to get down by the ladder, rung by rung. Finally you reach the same place. One who has jumped into the valley and one who has been coming down by a ladder, finally they reach the same point.

And remember : even descending by a ladder, when you come to the last rung, you jump! What will you do when you have come to the last rung? Your jump will be small, the other person's jump has been big — he jumped from the top of the hill, you jump only from the last rung. But the LAST moment is ALWAYS of jump. It cannot be otherwise.

Whether you follow the gradual path or the sudden — the sudden is, of course, a pathless path, a gateless gate — whatsoever you follow, finally, at the last moment, the quantum leap has to happen. It depends how much courage you have. If you have real courage to risk all, to stake all, to surrender all, it will happen THIS moment. If you are miserly, business-like, clever, cunning, conditional, then it will happen, slowly.

For the majority, growth groups are of immense importance. They prepare you, they help you to come to the point from where, even if you are not very courageous, you can take the jump. But the jump has to happen because you have to become discontinuous with yourself.

Don't see any conflict between these two. It has always been thought that there is a conflict between the sudden and the gradual. This may be the first place in the world where the sudden and the gradual are meeting. Otherwise, those who have been teaching sudden enlightenment... Hui Neng. Of course, Hui Neng became suddenly enlightened — how can he teach you gradual enlightenment? And his followers, although they are not enlightened they go on talking about sudden enlightenment, and they are against the gradual, antagonistic to the idea of gradual growth.

And the people like, for example, Patanjali, who have grown from a seed to a big tree, not like a jump, who have grown like a small child growing towards youth, step by step — he charts the whole map : from the body to the mind, from the mind to the soul, from the soul to the infinite. He charts the WHOLE process; he is gradual. Now, he will be against Hui Neng, because when Patanjali talks about the eight limbs of Yoga, Hui Neng talks only about the eighth — samadhi — the seven are dropped, the seven are not included at all. For Hui Neng, those seven are a kind of postponement : Why waste time with yoga asanas — yoga postures — what are you doing? Enlightenment has nothing to do with the body. In what posture you are, enlightenment has nothing to do with that. You can be standing on your head, you can be sitting Buddhalike, you can be lying down — it can happen! It can happen in any posture because it is not a physical phenomenon at all.

No yoga posture has any relevance! certainly not for Hui Neng, because he was passing through the market, somebody else was reading the Diamond Sutra, he simply heard it... and hearing it, it happened. There is no question of any yoga posture. There is no question of a certain diet. There is no question of any practice of breathing. All the seven limbs are dropped; only the eighth — samadhi, ecstasy.... He immediately became ecstatic. It happened to him, so he is right; he says, "It has happened to me — it can happen to you, it can happen to everybody. Why waste your time practising unnecessary things? All else is arbitrary. The essential is samadhi."

Now, Patanjali knows differently. Samadhi has not happened immediately to him; he has been growing towards it, slowly, slowly. It has been a growth — not only of one life, but many lives. It has been gradual, it has been slow; it has been like a seed becoming a tree. And he will say, "Don't listen to such people — these people are mad. Things don't happen like that! No seed has ever been known to suddenly become a great cedar of Lebanon — no seed has ever been known to. This Hui Neng has gone mad!"

Or, Patanjali will find some way to explain it. He will say, "Hui Neng must have been doing all the other things in his past lives; he was ready — he had fulfilled the seven limbs in his past lives. That's why suddenly the eighth has happened, but the eighth CANNOT happen unless those seven have been fulfilled. Hui Neng LOOKS sudden, but is not sudden."

And ask Hui Neng, "What about Patanjali?" and he will say, "He is befooling himself. The thing could have happened directly — he was unnecessarily going round and round. He could have jumped." And the difference.... Hui Neng will say, "Man is not a seed — man is already a cedar of Lebanon. Just forgotten! If man is a seed, then time is a must to become a tree" — but Hui Neng's whole point is : "Man is ALREADY the tree. Just fallen asleep. In sleep dreaming that 'I am a seed'. He has to be simply shocked and awakened. Just the dream has to be broken. Once the tree opens its eyes, it will KNOW that there is no need for any growth."

For Patanjali, 'becoming' is the most valuable word; for Hui Neng, 'being' is the most valuable word.

To me, both are true. I am a bridge between Patanjali and Hui Neng. And I understand : Hui Neng is ultimately true, but 'ultimately' true; and very rarely will you be able to find a person who becomes enlightened by hearing four lines... it is not easy to find such a person. But it is possible; I don't say it is impossible.

For ninety-nine percent, Patanjali will be the way. So I don't discard Patanjali — I don't discard anything. Everything is accepted and used. Use all the methods skillfully and you will be benefited by all. And don't become obsessed with a method. Don't say that "I believe in gradual growth." If you say, "I believe in gradual growth," then you are preventing the possibility of sudden enlightenment. Maybe you are the person — who knows? — you are Hui Neng! Even Hui Neng was not aware until he became enlightened. Who knows?! Somebody may be here who is a Hui Neng, a potential Hui Neng, and if he starts thinking that "No, it is not possible. I don't believe in sudden enlightenment," that very idea will prevent him. Then he will listen to the four lines of the Diamond Sutra and will not become enlightened because of his idea.

I would like you to remain open.

But I am not saying that everybody is going to become enlightened just by listening to those four lines of the Diamond Sutra, because then there is again a danger : listening to those four lines, you may start believing you have become enlightened. That will be a pretension, that will be delirium, that will be madness. Both dangers are there.

I make you aware of all the dangers, all the possibilities; I make all the paths available to you.

Don't believe in any path. Don't discard any path offhand, a priori, no. Keep open. And use whatsoever feels right in this moment. And everything will help and everything will support and everything will strengthen, and everything will open you up. All things can be used. And you can be benefited by all the paths.

The second question :

I am frustrated — you say be herenow, drop the mind, be spontaneous — to me this would be an enlightened state. I don't experience being enlightened, so what does this asshole do in the meantime?

MEANTIME, ENJOY BEING UNENLIGHTENED — because, who knows, tomorrow you may become enlightened. I make you beware : meanwhile enjoy being unenlightened — because once enlightened, you are enlightened forever. Watch out! Then don't come to me and say that "Now I have become enlightened and I want to enjoy things which only can be enjoyed in a state of unenlightenment." Then I will not be of much help.

I can help you from unenlightenment towards enlightenment; I cannot help you from enlightenment towards unenlightenment.

That is not possible. That has never happened! That is not possible — once you know, you know. Then a thousand and one things will immediately become impossible. So don't waste time — enjoy!

You ask me : I AM FRUSTRATED...

Because you are carrying an idea of becoming enlightened — and you are unenlightened! And the idea of becoming enlightened is continuously hammering, and continuously you know you are unenlightened, so frustration....

You misunderstand me. You continuously misunderstand me. I am not giving you a goal, enlightenment is not a goal. Naturally, you will ask, "Then how does it come?" If you can start enjoying your unenlightened state, it will come on its own — enjoyment bridges both. That's why my emphasis is on joy, celebration, happiness — because happiness bridges both.

The unenlightened person can also be happy, and the enlightened person is necessarily happy. That is the only quality that they share; that is the only quality that overlaps. I have not come across any other quality that overlaps. Hence, I say : The quality that overlaps can be used as a bridge.

The unenlightened person can be joyous only momentarily — obviously, because his mind is wavering. He is continuously dragged to the past, to the future, here and there, and he cannot remain here. But for moments he can... just coming from the past and going to the future, he can for a moment be in the present. Coming from the future, going to the past, he can have a halt, just a little holiday in the present. He passes many times in the day, again and again; he shuttles back and forth. Shuttling back and forth he crosses the present many times. In those fragmentary spaces he can be happy. His happiness cannot be eternal. But happiness IS happiness, eternal or momentary.

When you are dancing and celebrating, your dance and celebration has the same quality as when Kabir is dancing or Meera is dancing — the SAME quality. The difference is of quantity, not of quality. It is only momentary; it comes and it goes. It does not stay; it is like a flash. By the time you become aware of it, it is gone. But it is the same thing!

It becomes a sun to a Kabir, to a Meera; it becomes a constant source of light. But lightning in the clouds has the SAME quality — it is not different. It is the SAME light —although you cannot read a book, and you cannot write a letter. By the time you take the pen in your hand, the lightning is gone and it is deep darkness. But still, remember, the quality of fire, the quality of electricity is the same — whether it is a constant source like the sun or a very momentary flash of lightning, the difference is only of time.

Happiness overlaps. When Buddha is, he is happy, he is simply happy; it remains. It is like breathing; it is a climate around him — it never leaves him. To you it comes like a fragrance : for a moment your nostrils are full of it and the next moment it is gone and you are full of the stink of the world — but it is the same fragrance. In Buddha's life the flower has bloomed, in your life the flower has not bloomed — it comes and goes.

You are feeling frustrated because this idea of enlightenment is becoming a heavy phenomenon for you. You are making a goal out of it, and you will create misery. And a miserable person can never become enlightened.

Drop misery!... And you will ask : "How to drop misery?" Drop goals. Goals create misery. When you are hankering for something and you cannot get it, you become miserable. When you don't hanker for anything, but start moving in a new dimension, whatsoever you have, you start enjoying it.... You may be sitting in the small garden of your cottage and thinking of the great palace — how to get it? In that very idea of the great palace which you can see far away in the sunlight, the marble palace, you are becoming miserable. The more you become focussed on THAT palace, the more you forget the beauties of this small cottage — the flowers are there, the lawn is green, the trees are happy, the wind is blowing, the sun is showering, the birds are singing.... For the birds there's not much difference between a palace and a hut. And the flowers bloom the same, and the sun showers the same — on the just, on the unjust, on the poor, on the rich, on the beautiful, on the ugly, on the successful, on the failures.

You are missing.

Forget the palace! In forgetting the palace, you will not be miserable. Start moving with this bird that is blessing you, sitting on your small tree singing a song. Listen to it! And these rays of the sun that are falling on you, rejoice! sing a song! dance with the trees! Lie down on the grass; feel the wetness of it and the aliveness of it.

That's what I mean : Meanwhile enjoy your unenlightenment.

And if you can enjoy your unenlightenment, you will be surprised that the hut has become a palace. You will be surprised by the transformation that happens around you — because it has happened inside you. When you change, the whole world changes.

If you can enjoy your unenlightened state, enlightenment is going to happen to you. It cannot happen by desiring — it happens only by rejoicing. Jesus says again and again : Rejoice! Rejoice! Why? There is a key, a golden key : if you can rejoice, you will become capable of more rejoicings. If you can rejoice, your heart will dance, throb, will be able to open more... and more will be coming.

You always get that for which you are ready. More you cannot get.

You say : I AM FRUSTRATED. YOU SAY BE HERENOW, DROP THE MIND, BE SPONTANEOUS...

You go on misunderstanding me. When I say to you, "Be spontaneous," you make a goal out of it — and that's what I am saying not to do, please. Be spontaneous means don't have any goals. You make a goal out of being spontaneous. You start trying : How to be spontaneous? The moment you bring 'how', you can never be spontaneous, because there is no how to it. How always leads into the future. How always prepares, plans. How can you plan to be spontaneous? Spontaneity is an understanding that "I have not to run after the desires." Seeing the futility of desires, one no more runs after them and there is spontaneity.

When I say drop the mind, you start trying to drop the mind. Who is trying? The mind starts trying to drop the mind itself. Now, this is impossible — the mind cannot drop the mind. You have to understand these things!

What I am teaching you here is not something that has to be done : it is something that has to be understood. And you are much too interested in doing. You are in such a hurry to do something that you don't listen to what I am saying, you don't get the point, and immediately you start planning how to drop the mind. Now, WHO is this planning? Who is this thinking how to drop the mind? It is the mind itself. Now a new desire has arisen in you of dropping the mind — now a new marble palace, now a new goal.

Mind is desiring. Mind is goal-orientation.

To drop the mind means : see the point! that mind leads you astray; it never allows you to be herenow. Seeing that, be finished with goals. Seeing that, don't create new goals of dropping the mind and being spontaneous and being herenow. Seeing the point, have a good laugh... relax, rejoice. And you are herenow, and in the herenow there is no mind. And when there is no mind, there is spontaneity. Meanwhile, enjoy!

I DON'T EXPERIENCE BEING ENLIGHTENED.

You will never experience being enlightened. How can YOU experience being enlightened? You are the barrier. And enlightenment is not an experience — because there is no experiencer in it. Enlightenment is experiencing, not experience. In experience there is division — the experiencer, the experienced. Between the two exists experience. When the experiencer and the experienced are no more separate, they have melted into each other, when the observer has become the observed, when the knower and the known are no more separate, then there is a totally new phenomenon for which I would like to use the word 'experiencing'. I would like to use a verb: experiencing.

Experience is a noun, closed, finished. Experiencing is ongoing, it is riverlike. Those two, the duality of the knower and the known, have dissolved into the river. There is nobody who knows enlightenment, and there is not anything like enlightenment which can be known as an object.

Forget about these complex things. Simply start enjoying. That simple thing can be done easily — you can dance, you can sing, you can love, you can eat, you can go for a walk, you can have a good sleep. All these activities are beautiful if you can be totally in them, dissolved.

Mind will go on trying its ways on you, its tricks on you. And you will be led astray by the mind many times. Whenever you remember, again have a good laugh, rejoice. Don't start fighting with the mind. Neglect. Ignore. This is just an old habit. Watch. Don't pay much attention.

By not giving attention, slowly, slowly you will starve the mind. It will start shrinking. One day, it will not be there. When the mind is gone, you are gone. When you are gone, there is enlightenment.

You say: I DON'T EXPERIENCE BEING ENLIGHTENED, SO WHAT DOES THIS ASSHOLE DO IN THE MEANTIME?

You ARE enlightenment... you have simply forgotten it. A remembrance will come to you — not by your effort, but by being in tune with existence.

An old boxer phoned his manager. "Harry," he said, "you gotta ged me anudder fight, I wanna fight Slasher Delaney."

"No, boy," replied Harry. "You're over the hill, no more fights. How many times do I hafta tell ya?"

"But please Harry; just this one, I know I can beat 'im. Please Harry, one more fight!"

"No! You're past it. Quit while you're still on yer feet. You can't fight again."

"But Harry," pleaded the old fighter, "why can't I fight Slasher Delaney?"

"Why can't you fight Slasher Delaney?" yelled the manager, "because, you stupid shit, you are Slasher Delaney!"

Third question :

Although I have been standing on my head for lifetimes, I cannot walk without feet. Why?

YOU CAN GO ON STANDING ON YOUR HEAD FOR MANY more lifetimes... that has nothing to do with it. To walk without feet you need not stand on your head. That has no relevance. It has no relationship.

To walk without feet and to fly without wings, you need not do any unnecessary things like standing on your head. Standing on your head you will not even be able to walk with your feet — what to say about walking without feet? Standing on your head you will not be able to walk at all. Standing on your head you will be dead, you will not be alive.

When I say walk without feet, what am I saying? I am saying, first : learn how to walk with feet, and then be very very watchful inside, be alert. Create a luminous consciousness. See who is walking when you are walking. Are you really walking? You have come from England to India, or from Japan to India — has anything really moved inside you? You have not walked. The body has been carried from Japan to India, but your consciousness is the same.

You were a child; now you are a young man or an old man, you have walked a long way — but have you really changed? Deep at the very core of your being you have not walked at all; there has been no journey. You are exactly the same at the very core of your being.

Walking, if you watch, you will know there is no walking. Talking, if you watch, you will see there is no talking. Thinking, if you watch, you will see there is no thinking. The deepest core of your being remains untouched, untouchable. It is a lotus in the water — remains in the water but untouched.

Knowing that witness is what I mean...

THINK WITHOUT MIND
FLY WITHOUT WINGS
WALK WITHOUT FEET

I am not teaching you some circus tricks here — that you can fly, so stand on your head.

A circus manager was interviewing people for jobs in his circus. By the end of the day he had hired very few and turned down many, while getting very bored with all their tricks. As he was ready to leave his office, a man walked in and said, "I would like to get a job in your circus."

Without giving him a glance, the manager asked, "And what can you do?"

"I can fly like a bird," said the man.

"Sorry, we have no need for that, and all jobs are taken," said the manager.

"Oh well," said the man, disappointed — and flew out of the window.

But, Parinirvana, I am not teaching those tricks here. You have to drop all tricks — these are all tricks! People become very much interested, because ego feels very much fulfilled if you can do something which nobody else can do : if you can walk without feet, if you can fly without wings, you will feel greatly happy — although you have not achieved anything! Stupid birds are flying, so what have you achieved? There is no achievement in it.

It happened : a man came to Ramakrishna, and he was very haughty and very arrogant, and he said, "Do you know? — I can walk on the river." They were sitting on the bank of the Ganges in Dakshineshwar. Ramakrishna laughed. He was a very very innocent man. He said, "You can walk on the river?"

And the man said, "Yes."

And Ramakrishna said, "How many years did it take you to learn the trick?"

He said, "Eighteen years."

Ramakrishna laughed; said, "You fool — eighteen years?! When I want to go to the other side, just two paise... something worth two paise — eighteen years?! I have never come across such a fool," he said. "You have wasted your life! I just go by the ferryboat. There is no need...!"

But these things attract; the mind becomes very much interested if something miraculous can happen to you. And miracles are happening continuously, but you don't see them — that you are breathing, that you are alive, that you are loving, that you are seeing the sunrays, the sky, that the world is such a benediction. Miracles are happening every moment! But you would like to fly like a stupid bird, and then you will feel very good that you have become a great yogi or something.

Remember : be ordinary; don't try to be special in any way, otherwise you will be moving in a wrong direction. To be special means to be egoistic, and ego is the only problem. There is no other problem. Forget about being special. Just be ordinary. And there is great joy in being ordinary. Just be human.

And by being ordinary you will come to know — you will know the art of walking without feet and flying without wings. That art simply means that "I am not the doer. I have relaxed. Now God walks in me, God talks in me, God loves through me, but I am a hollow bamboo. I have no special goal in life — His goal is my goal. And if He has no goals, I am perfectly happy with no goal. I am flowing with the river. Wherever it leads, that is my home — if it leads anywhere. If it doesn't lead anywhere, then that is my home."

This is relaxation. And to relax in reality is to attain, is to be enlightened. Enlightenment is an utter let-go.

The fourth question :

If people have been so much destroyed by guilt, as you say they have been, then how do they manage to live at all?

I ALSO WONDER! It is a great mystery, a riddle, how they manage to live at all. Their sources of life are poisoned. In fact, they are not living — they are only managing to live. Managing to live is not living. Managing to live is just somehow dragging, pretending; it is pseudo, phoney.

All your life sources have been poisoned. And unless you get rid of the priest and the politician, you will never be able to really live. At the most you can manage. But by managing you can only postpone death, you cannot really live. You can go on postponing death one day more, one day more — but this is not life!

Life needs passion. Life needs intensity. Life needs fire — because only when fire is there and flame is there do you bloom; otherwise, you are just lukewarm, so-so.

What is your love? How can you LOVE? For five thousand years love has been condemned, so much so that even if you think that you are no more part of any church, that you don't go to the priest, it doesn't matter much. The poisoning has gone so deep in the blood, in the bones and the marrow that even if you don't go to the church, the church continues in you; deep down it goes on pulling you, controlling you.

Still you manage! Still one has to love and one has to live, so one lives and one loves, but love creates only agony, not ecstasy. And each agony proves that the priest is right. And the priest is the cause of the agony! That is the beauty of the whole thing. But each time you feel the agony of it, you are reminded again that the priest was right, that love is misery.

Love is not misery! Love is sheer joy. But it has been contaminated, polluted, so many things have been forced into it, that it is no more love, it is something else. Each time you feel frustration, the priest stands proved : "He was right, I was wrong; I should have listened. I should have been wiser." Each love relationship proves the priest was right, because no love relationship is a love relationship at all. It is possessiveness, it is jealousy, it is domination, it is anger, it is violence — it is hatred.

The very idea that you possess a person is the ugliest that you can invent. Psychological monopoly destroys all love, and when love is destroyed, naturally you feel in agony, because the ecstasy is missing and you invested so much for the ecstasy. And the ecstasy is not there and you are left crushed, in a collapse. Deep down, the priest speaks : "Listen, I have been telling you — had I not told you before that love is illusory? that love is misery? that love brings anguish? Be alert in future. Escape!"

The priest has made you so much against life. He could not destroy life completely, that is true. He cannot. It is like a tree, but you have poisoned the roots. He could not destroy life; life is irrepressible, life is divine, life is God. The priest was impotent to kill it completely, but at least he succeeded in poisoning lt.

I have heard :

At a mountain resort, a man who was on vacation without his wife, and a woman who was on vacation without her husband, met at table. After a few days of pleasant conversation, they both grew fond of each other and eventually found themselves in bed together. But they felt very guilty and conscience-stricken.

"My wife," said the errant husband, "works and slaves to make a nice home for my children." And he burst into tears.

"My husband is so good to me," said the cheating wife. "He is working his fingers to the bone to send me on vacation, and I wind up in bed with a lover." And then she burst into tears too.

This kept on for five days. So what happened? They spent the whole week long making love and crying, and crying and making love.

This is what is happening all over the world. You cannot go totally into anything. You cannot escape totally either. You are hanging in the middle; you don't belong to this side and you don't belong to that side. You cannot escape from love, because when you escape from love you feel utterly lonely and there is misery. That misery is brought by nature, because nature intends you to relate; nature intends you to fall in tune with the total, and to fall in tune with the total you have to start with individuals.

Individuals are the doors for the total. So if you escape to the Himalayan caves or to a Catholic monastery, nature will take revenge, nature will never forgive you. You will be lonely, sad; your life will be a kind of vegetation. You will vegetate. Your prayers will also be dull, because without a loving heart how can prayers be alive? Your reading of the Bible or the Diamond Sutra will not have any flame, because when love dies, all flame dies. You will be just dragging, dull, dead. You will somehow live, waiting for death. Death will be your delivery. Life will be a constant burden.

Nature will take revenge and nature will tell you, "Go back to life. Relate with people. Life is in relationship and joy is in relationship. Go and love! Prayer arises out of love. Merged in love, one comes to experience meditation for the first time. Go into life!" Life will go on goading you. Life cannot leave you so easily. It never leaves. It has never left anybody!

So you will be miserable. Your only joy will be one, that you are going to paradise and heaven and there you will enjoy all things, and all these worldly people, these are going to hell and they will be burnt. And your only joy will be this fantasy, that everybody else who is enjoying in the world is going to hell. You can have a vicarious enjoyment. It is a kind of sadism. You want the whole world to go to hell; just because YOU are suffering, you would like everybody else to suffer. You are angry; deep down you are envious and jealous. You cannot forgive these people who are dancing in the streets, who are making love, who are living, who are singing songs. Those songs go on floating in the monastery. You have to take revenge.

Hell is created by the monks just as a kind of revenge. Hell exists not. It is a pure invention of those who have left life and cannot enjoy their seclusion. And for themselves they have created a heaven. In the heaven they will enjoy all the things that they have left here — ALL the things!

In the Mohammedan paradise, wine flows in rivers. Here they have left wine; in the paradise they will be rewarded a thousandfold, a millionfold. In heaven there are beautiful women who never go beyond eighteen. They are stuck there; their growth stops. Eighteen is the only age. And their beauty is not the ordinary beauty of this world, not muddy; they don't smell of sweat, they are fragrant. They have bodies of gold.

Mm? — these are fantasies. These people have missed women here; now they are fantasizing. They are somehow consoling themselves : "Just wait a little more. Death will come and you will be delivered, and God is going to repay you infinitely." They have done a great job because they have left life. And life is persistent inside them — that life is creating fantasies.

When you fast your hunger creates fantasies of eating. When you become a celibate, a forced celibate, your hunger for the warmth of a woman or a man's body creates fantasies. If you escape, life will not forgive you, nature will not forgive you, God will not forgive you! You have gone against God, because this life is God's : if you go against life, you go against its creator.

If you don't escape and you don't listen to the priest, and you go against the priest, the priest will never forgive you. So whenever you are with a woman, the priest is there inside destroying the joy of it. He is creating your so-called conscience, morality, puritanism; he is condemning you there. And you start self-condemning. And because you can't go deep into love, this priest is pulling you back, love becomes agony. Rather than becoming an ecstasy it turns into an agony — then the priest is proved right. And you start thinking about how to go into a monastery, how to leave all this love.

The priest cannot forgive you if you are alive. And if you

become dead in a monastery, life cannot forgive you. You are in this dilemma.

Listen to life and not to the priest. The priest has been in the service of the Devil; he is Satan's disciple. Listen to life. Go deep in life. If love brings misery, then find out —it cannot be love. Something else is pretending to be love, something else is masquerading as love. Analyze it, and drop all that is not love from love. And, slowly slowly, you will start moving towards prayer and meditation.

The last question :

Why am I so much fascinated by pornography?

MUST BE YOUR RELIGIOUS UPBRINGING — Sunday school; otherwise, there is no need to be interested in pornography. When you are against the real, you start imagining.

The day religious upbringing disappears from the earth, pornography will die. It cannot die before it.

This looks very paradoxical. Magazines like *Playboy* exist only with the support of the Vatican. Without the Pope there will be no *Playboy* magazine; it cannot exist. It will not have any reason to exist. The priest is behind it.

Why should you be interested in pornography when alive people are here? And it is so beautiful to look at alive people. You don't become interested in the picture of a naked tree, do you? because all trees are naked! Just do one thing : cover all the trees... and sooner or later you will find magazines circulating underground — naked trees! And people will be reading them, putting them inside their Bibles and looking at them and enjoying. Try it and you will see.

Pornography can disappear only when people accept their nudity naturally. You don't want to see cats and dogs and lions and tigers naked in pictures — they ARE naked! In fact, when a dog passes you, you don't even recognize the fact; you don't take note of it that he is naked. There are a few ladies in England, I have heard, who cover their dogs with clothes. They are afraid — the nudity of the dog may disturb some religious, spiritual soul.

I have heard, Bertrand Russell has written in his autobiography that in his childhood days those were the days, Victorian days — that even the legs of the chairs were covered, because they are LEGS.

Let man be natural and pornography disappears. Let people be nude... not that they have to sit nude in their offices; there is no need to go that far. But on the beaches, on the rivers, or when they are at ease, relaxing in their homes, resting under the sun in their gardens, they should be nude! Let children play around nude, around nude mother and father. Pornography will disappear! Who will look at the *Playboy* magazine? for what? Something is being deprived, some natural curiosity is being deprived, hence pornography.

You ask : WHY AM I SO MUCH FASCINATED BY PORNOGRAPHY?

You will be surprised to know that the word 'fascinated' comes from the word 'phallus'. Man has been pathologically fascinated by the phallus — for NO reason. The only reason is that people have been hiding it. Even if you go to a nude primitive community, the WHOLE body is nude, but the sexual organ they will hide — so at least that much pornography will continue.

Why this fear? How did it come? It must have a deep root cause somewhere in the past, maybe lost to human consciousness, but it is there.

The word 'phallus' in its turn comes from a Sanskrit root *phala. Phala* means the fruit. Reaching to the roots of this word 'fascination' is very paying : first it comes from 'phallus', and 'phallus' comes from *phala; phala* means fruit, bearing fruit. Man became aware that the sexual organ is the most important organ because it gives birth to life; he became aware that somehow life must be residing in it. It is precious — hide it! It is a treasure.

Don't let anybody see it. Somebody may take your treasure, somebody may steal it, somebody may harm it.

This idea got deep into the unconsciousness of man. There is no reality behind it. There is no reason. Pornography is a by-product. And the priest became aware of one thing — it was obvious — that people fall in love and they forget the whole thing, the whole world. Falling in love, or making love, they simply disappear from this world, they move into another dimension. And that dimension is the priest's dimension — he wants monopoly over it. He does not want any other way for you to approach God; he wants you to come through the right way that he provides : the prayer, the meditation, this and that. And he became aware that people have a natural key with them, a natural door opens into the divine — that has to be stopped. Otherwise who will be interested in their prayer and in their meditations? Who will be interested in churches and temples? First people's natural capacity to enter into God has to be stopped and destroyed, then the profession can flourish.

That's how it has happened.

Get rid of the priest within you, say goodbye. And then suddenly you will see that pornography has disappeared. Kill the priest in your unconscious and you will see a great change happening in your being. You will be more together.

A small beautiful story for you to meditate...

Three priests went to Grand Central Station to get a train to Buffalo. The older two appointed the youngest one to go to the counter to buy three tickets. Behind the wicket stood a gorgeously buxom young lady wearing a dress of outrageous décolleté. The young priest was visibly flustered.

Finally, he blurted out, "Please let me have three pickets for Titsburgh."

When he realized what he had said, he was mortified, and ran back to the other two priests.

The second took the money and approached the window. Here he too encountered the same upset, but managed to say,

"Can I have three tickets for Pittsburgh?" And then, laying down a $50 bill, he continued, "And I would like my change in nipples and dimes."

Realizing what he had said, he was so abashed he left the tickets on the counter and ran back to the other two priests.

The third, the eldest, then strode up to the counter to ask for the tickets and the change. Regarding at length the female clerk dressed in such a revealing fashion, he considered it his duty to admonish her.

"Young lady," he said, "you know if you go around dressed in such a provocative manner, you will most certainly obtain your just desserts in the life to come. It is my bounden duty to tell you that when you pass to the Great Beyond, St. Finger will certainly be there pointing his peter at you...."

CHAPTER
7

Any Moment!

The first question :

You implore us constantly to give up memory, to live in the herenow. But in giving up memory I must also give up my creative imagination, for I am a writer and all that I write about has its roots in what I remember I wonder — what would the world be like without art and the creative imagination that makes art possible? A Tolstoy could never become a Buddha, but then could a Buddha write War and Peace?

*P*RAMADA, YOU HAVE NOT UNDERSTOOD ME, but that's natural. It is impossible to understand me, because to understand me you will have to drop your memory. Your memory interferes. You only listen to my words, and then you go on interpreting those words according to your memory, according to your past. You cannot understand me if you are not herenow... only then the meeting. Only in that moment you ARE with me; otherwise, you are physically present here, psychologically absent.

I have not been telling you to drop your factual memory. That will be stupid! Your factual memory is a must. You MUST know your name, who your father is and who your mother is and who your wife is and who your child is and your address; you will have to go back to the hotel, you will have to find your room again. Factual memory is not meant — psychological memory is meant. Factual memory is not a problem, it is pure remembrance. When you become psychologically affected by it, then the problem arises. Try to understand the difference.

Yesterday somebody insulted you. Again he comes across you today. The factual memory is that "this man insulted me yesterday." The psychological memory is that seeing that man you become angry; seeing that man, you start boiling up. And the man may be coming just to ask for your apology; the man may be coming to be excused, to be forgiven. He may have realized his mistake; he may have realized his unconscious behaviour. He may be coming to befriend you again, but you become boiled up. You are angry, you start shouting. You don't see his face herenow; you go on being affected by the face which was yesterday. But yesterday is yesterday! How much water has flowed down the Ganges? This man is not the same man. Twenty-four hours have brought many changes.

And YOU are not the same man either.

The factual memory says, "This man insulted me yesterday," but that 'me' has changed. This man has changed. So it is as if that incident had happened between two persons with whom you have nothing to do any more — then you are psychologically free. You don't say, "I still feel angry." There is no lingering anger. Memory is there, but there is no psychological affectation. You meet the man again as he is now, and you meet him as you are now.

A man came and spat on Buddha's face. He was very angry. He was a Brahmin and Buddha was saying things which the priests were very angry about. Buddha wiped it off and asked the man, "Have you anything more to say?"

His disciple, Ananda, became very angry. He was so angry that he asked Buddha, "Just give me permission to put this man right. This is too much! I cannot tolerate it."

Buddha said, "But he has not spat on your face. This is my face. Secondly just look at the man! In what great trouble he is — just look at the man! Feel compassion for him. He wants to say something to me, but words are inadequate — that is my problem, my whole life's problem. And I see the man in the same situation. I want to relate things to you that I have come to know, but I cannot relate them because words are inadequate. And this man is in the same boat : he is so angry that no word can express his anger. Just as I am in so much love that no word, no act, can express it. I see this man's difficulty — hence he has spat. Just see!"

Buddha is seeing, Ananda is also seeing. Buddha is simply collecting a factual memory; Ananda is creating a psychological memory.

The man could not believe his ears, what Buddha was saying. He was very much shocked. He would not have been shocked if Buddha had hit him back, or Ananda had jumped upon him. There would have been no shock; that would have been expected, that would have been natural. That's how human beings react. But Buddha FEELING for the man, seeing his difficulty.... The man went, could not sleep the whole night, pondered over it, meditated over it. Started feeling a great hurt, started feeling what he had done. A wound opened in his heart.

Early in the morning, he rushed to Buddha's feet, fell down on Buddha's feet, kissed his feet. And Buddha said to Ananda, "Look, again the same problem! Now he is feeling so much for me, he cannot speak in words. He is touching my feet.

"Man is so helpless. Anything that is too much cannot be expressed, cannot be conveyed, cannot be communicated. Some gesture has to be found to symbolize it. Look!"

And the man started crying and he said, "Excuse me, sir. I am immensely sorry. It was absolute stupidity on my part to spit on you, a man like you."

Buddha said, "Forget about it! The man you spat upon is no more, and the man who spat is no more. You are new, I am new! Look — this sun that is rising is new. Everything is new. The yesterday is no more. Be finished with it! And how can I forgive? because you never spat on me. You spat on somebody who has departed."

Consciousness is a continuous river.

When I say drop your memory, I mean psychological memory; I don't mean factual memory. Buddha remembers perfectly that yesterday this man had spat on him, but he also remembers that neither this man is the same nor is he the same. That chapter is closed; it is not worth carrying it your whole life. But you go on carrying. Somebody had said something to you ten years before and you are still carrying it. Your mother was angry when you were a child and you are still carrying it. Your father had slapped you when you were just small and you are still carrying it, and you may be seventy years old.

These psychological memories go on burdening you. They destroy your freedom, they destroy your aliveness, they encage you. Factual memory is perfectly okay.

And one thing more to be understood : when there is no psychological memory, the factual memory is very accurate — because the psychological memory is a disturbance. When you are very much psychologically disturbed, how can you remember accurately? It is impossible! You are trembling, you are shaking, you are in a kind of earthquake — how can you remember exactly? You will exaggerate; you will add something, you will delete something, you will make something new out of it. You cannot be relied upon.

A man who has no psychological memory can be relied upon. That's why computers are more reliable than men, because they have no psychological memory. Just the facts — bare facts, naked facts. When you talk about a fact, then too it is not fact : much fiction has entered into it. You have moulded it, you have changed it, you have painted it, you have given it colours of your own — it is no more a fact! Only a Buddha, a Tathagata, an enlightened person, knows what a fact is; you never come across a fact, because you carry so many fictions in your mind. Whenever you find a fact, you immediately impose your fictions on it. You NEVER see that which is. You go on distorting reality.

Buddha says a Tathagata is always true, because he speaks in accordance with reality. A Tathagata speaks truth, never otherwise. A Tathagata is synonymous with suchness. Whatsoever it is, a Tathagata simply reflects it; it is a mirror.

That's what I mean : Drop psychological memories and you will become a mirror.

You have asked : YOU IMPLORE US CONSTANTLY TO GIVE UP MEMORY, TO LIVE IN THE HERE AND NOW.

That does not mean that your past cannot be remembered, because past is part of the present. Whatsoever you have been in the past, whatsoever you have done in the past, is PART of your present, it is HERE. Your child is in you, your young man is in you... all that you have been doing is in you. The food that you have eaten, it is past, but it has become your blood; it is circulating herenow; it has become your bone, it has become your marrow. The love that you went through may be past, but it has transformed you. It has given you a new vision of life; it has opened your eyes. Yesterday you were with me — it is past, but is it really totally past? How can it be totally past? You were changed by it; you were given a new spur, a new fire — that has become part of you.

Your present moment contains your whole past. And if you can understand me, your present moment also contains your whole future — because the past as it has happened has been changing you, it has been preparing you, and the future that is going to happen will happen the way you live in the present. The way you live herenow will have a great impact upon your future.

In the present moment all past is contained, and in the present moment all future is potential. But you need not be psychologically worried about it. It is already there! You need not carry it psychologically, you need not be burdened by it. If you understand me, that it is contained already... the tree is not thinking about the water that it soaked up yesterday, but it is there! thinking or not thinking. And the sunrays that fell on it yesterday, it is not thinking about them. Trees are not so foolish, not as stupid as men.

Why bother about the rays of yesterday? They have been absorbed, digested, they have become part — the green, the red and the gold. The tree is enjoying THIS morning's sun, with no psychological memory of yesterday. Although the yesterday is contained in the leaves, in the flowers, in the branches, in the roots, in the sap. It is contained! And the future is also coming : the new buds which will become flowers tomorrow are there. And the small new leaves which will become foliage tomorrow are there, on the way.

The present moment contains all. Now is eternity.

So I am not saying to forget the factual past; I am simply saying don't be disturbed by it any more. It should not be a psychological investment : it is a physical fact. Let it be so. And I am not saying become incapable of remembering it — it may be needed! When it is needed, the need is present, remember, and you have to respond to the need. Somebody asks you your phone number. The need is present because somebody is asking now, and you say, "How can I say my phone number? because I have dropped my past." Then you will get into unnecessary troubles; your life, rather than becoming free, rather than becoming a great joy and celebration, will be hampered at every step; you will find a thousand and one problems unnecessarily being created by you. There is no need.

Try to understand me.

And you say : BUT IN GIVING UP MEMORY I MUST ALSO GIVE UP MY CREATIVE IMAGINATION...

WHAT DOES MEMORY HAVE TO DO WITH CREATIVE IMAGINATION? In fact, the more memory you have, the less creative you will be — because you will go on repeating the memory! And creativity means allowing the new to happen. Allowing the new to happen means : put aside the memory so the past does not interfere. Let the new penetrate you. Let the new come and thrill your heart. The past will be needed, but not now; the past will be needed when you start expressing this new experience. Then the past will be needed, because the language will be needed — language comes from the past. You cannot invent language right now, or if you do invent it, it will be gibberish; it will not mean anything. And it will not be a communication; it will be talking in tongues, it will be baby talk. Not much creativity will come out of it. You will be talking nonsense.

To talk sense language is needed; language comes from the past. But language should come only when the experience has happened! Then use it as a technique. It should not hinder you.

When you see the rose opening in the early morning sun, SEE it, let it have an impact, ALLOW it to go deepest in you! Let its rosiness overpower you, overwhelm you. Don't say anything! Wait. Be patient. Be open. Absorb. Let the rose reach you, and you reach to the rose. Let there be a meeting, a communion of two beings — the rose and you. Let there be a penetration, an interpenetration.

And remember : the deeper the rose goes in you, the deeper you can go into the rose; it is always in the same proportion. A moment comes when you don't know who is the rose and who is the spectator. A moment comes when you become the rose and the rose becomes you, when the observer is the observed, when all duality disappears. In THAT moment you will know the reality, the suchness of the rose. Then, catch hold of your language, catch hold of your art. If you are a painter, then take your brush and colour and your canvas, and paint it. If you are a poet, then rush into your factual memory for right words so that you can express this experience.

But WHILE the experience is happening, don't go on talking inside yourself. The inner talk will be an interference. You will never know the rose in its intensity and depth. You will know only the superficial, the shallow. And if you know the shallow, the shallow is going to be your expression; your art will not be of much value.

You ask me : BUT IN GIVING UP MEMORY I MUST ALSO GIVE UP MY CREATIVE IMAGINATION...

You don't understand the meaning of 'creative'. Creative means the new, the novel, the original; creative means the fresh, the unknown. You have to be open for it, vulnerable for it.

Put aside the memory. Its use is later on. Right now it will be an interference.

Right now, for instance, you are listening to me — put your memory aside. When you are listening to me, are you repeating inside yourself all the mathematics that you know? Are you counting figures inside? Are you repeating geography that you know? Are you repeating history that you know? You have put them aside. Do the same with language too, as you do with history and mathematics and geography. Do the same with language — do the same with your memory! Put it aside! It will be needed, but when it is needed, only then use it. Put the WHOLE mind aside!

You are not destroying the mind : you are simply giving it a rest. It is not needed. You can give it a holiday. You can say to the mind, "Rest for one hour and let me listen. And when I have listened, when I have absorbed, when I have eaten and drunk, then I will recall you, then your help will be needed — your language, your knowledge, your information will be needed. Then I am going to paint a picture or write a poem, or write a book, but RIGHT now, you can rest." And the mind will be more fresh after a rest. You don't allow the mind rest, that's why your mind remains mediocre.

Just think of a man who wants to participate in an Olympic race, and he continuously goes on running twenty-four hours a day preparing for an Olympic race. By the time the race happens he will not even be able to move, he will be so dead tired. Before the race, you will have to rest, you will have to get AS deep a rest as possible so the body is rejuvenated.

Exactly the same has to be done with the mind. Creative imagination has nothing to do with memory only then is it creative. If you understand me, and you drop psychological memory, you will become creative. Otherwise, what you call creation is not really creation — it is just a composition. There is a great difference between creation and composition. You go on arranging your old known things in different ways, but they are old; nothing is new there. You simply manage to change the structure.

It is like arranging your drawing-room : the furniture is the same, the pictures on the wall are the same, the curtains are the same, but you can arrange again. You can put this chair there and that table here, and you can change this picture from this wall to the other. It may look new, but it is not new. It is a composition; you have not created anything.

That's what ninety-nine percent of authors, poets, painters, go on doing. They are mediocre; they are not creative.

The creative person is one who brings something from the unknown into the world of the known, who brings something from God into the world, who helps God to utter something; who becomes a hollow bamboo and allows God to flow through him. How can you become a hollow bamboo? If you are too full of the mind, you cannot become a hollow bamboo. And creativity is from the creator. Creativity is not of you or from you. You disappear, then the creativity is — when the creator takes possession of you.

The real creators know it perfectly well, that they are not the creators — they were just instrumental, they were mediums. Something happened through them, true, but they are not the doers of it.

Remember the difference between a technician and a creative person. A technician just knows how to do a thing. Maybe he knows perfectly how to do a thing, but he has no insight. A creative person is one who has insight, who can see things which nobody has ever seen before — who can see things which no eye has ever been able to see — who hears things which nobody has heard before. Then there is creativity.

Just see.... Jesus' statements are creative — nobody has spoken like that before. He is not an educated person. He knows nothing of the skill; he knows nothing about eloquence — but he is eloquent as rarely very few people ever have been. What is his secret? He has insight. He has looked into God. He has looked into the unknown. He has encountered the unknown and the unknowable. He has been into that space; from that space he brings a few fragments. Only fragments can be brought, but when you bring some fragments from the unknowable you transform the whole quality of human consciousness on the earth.

He IS creative. I will call him the artist. Or a Buddha, or a Krishna, or a Lao Tzu — these are real artists! They make the impossible happen. The impossible is the meeting of the known

with the unknown, the meeting of the mind with the no-mind —
that is the impossible. They make it happen.

You say : BUT IN GIVING UP MEMORY I MUST ALSO GIVE UP
MY CREATIVE IMAGINATION...

No. That has nothing to do with creative imagination. In fact,
if you put your memory aside, you will have creative imagination.
You cannot have creative imagination if you are too much
burdened by the memory.

You say : FOR I AM A WRITER AND ALL THAT I WRITE ABOUT
HAS ITS ROOTS IN WHAT I REMEMBER.

Then you are not much of a writer. Then you go on writing
about the past. Then you go on writing memoirs. You don't bring
the future in. You go on writing records. You are a file-keeper!
You CAN become a writer, but then you will have to make contact
with the unknown — not that which you remember. The
remembered is already dead. You will have to make contact with
that which is, not that which you remember. You will have to
make contact with the suchness that surrounds you. You will have
to go deep into the present so that something of the past also
can be caught in your net.

The real creativity is not out of remembrance but out of
consciousness. You will have to become MORE conscious. The
more conscious you are, the bigger the net you have, and of
course the more fish will be caught.

You say : I WONDER — WHAT WOULD THE WORLD BE LIKE
WITHOUT ART AND THE CREATIVE IMAGINATION THAT
MAKES ART POSSIBLE?

Ninety-nine percent of art is just not art at all. It is rubbish.
Rarely is there a work of art, very rarely. Others are just imitators,
technicians, skillful people, clever people, but not artists. And that
ninety-nine percent of art disappearing from the earth will be a
blessing — because it is more like a vomit rather than anything
creative.

NOW there is something very meaningful around : art therapy.

It is meaningful! It has got the point. When people are ill, mentally ill, art can be of help. A mentally ill person can be given canvasses and colours and brush and told to paint whatsoever he wants to paint. Of course, whatsoever he paints will be mad, maddening. But after painting a few mad things, you will be surprised that he is coming back to sanity. That painting has been like a catharsis; it was a vomit. His system has thrown it out.

NOW, the so-called modern art is nothing but that. Picasso's paintings may have saved Picasso from becoming mad, but that's all there is to it. And they are dangerous for you to meditate upon because if you meditate upon somebody's vomit, you will go mad. Avoid! Never keep a Picasso painting in your bedroom, otherwise you will have nightmares.

Just think : keep the Picasso painting for fifteen minutes in front of you and go on looking at it... and you will start feeling restlessness, discomfort, giddy, nauseous. What is happening? It is somebody's vomit! It has helped him, it was good for him, but it is not good for others.

Look at a Michelangelo and you can meditate for hours. And the more you meditate, the more silent and peaceful you will become. It is not a vomit. He has brought something from the unknown. It is not his madness that he has thrown out of his system through the painting or through the sculpture or through the poetry or through music. It is NOT that he was ill and that he wanted to get rid of his illness. No. It was just the opposite : he was pregnant, not ill. He was pregnant — pregnant with God. Something had taken root into his being and he wanted to share it. It is a fruitfulness, a fulfillment. He has LIVED in a creative way. He has LOVED life in a creative way. He has allowed life to enter into his deepest shrine, and there he has become pregnant with life — or pregnant with God. And when you are pregnant you have to give birth.

Picasso is vomiting. Michelangelo is giving birth. Nietzsche is vomiting. Buddha is giving birth. There is AS much difference between these two as there can be. To give birth to a child is one thing and to vomit is another. Beethoven is giving birth. Something immensely valuable is descending through him. Listening to his music you will be transformed, you will be transported into another world. He will give you a few glimpses of the other shore.

Ninety-nine percent of modern art is pathological. If it disappears from the world, it will be very very healthy, it will be helpful. It will not harm. The modern mind is an angry mind — angry because you cannot contact your being, angry because you have lost all meaning, angry because you don't know what significance is.

One of the famous books of Jean Paul Sartre is *Nausea*. That is the state of the modern mind; the modern mind is nauseous, in a great torture. And the torture is its own creation.

Friedrich Nietzsche declared God is dead. The day he declared God is dead, he started becoming insane — because by your declaration that God is dead... GOD cannot be dead just by your declaration. Your declaration does not make any difference. But the moment Nietzsche started believing this, that God is dead, HE started dying, he started losing sanity. A world without God is bound to be an insane world — because a world without God will not have any context in which to become significant.

Just watch.... You read a poem; those words in the poem have meaning only in the context of the poem. If you take a word out of the context, it has no meaning. It was so beautiful IN the context! You cut out a piece of a painting — and it has no meaning, because it has lost its roots in the context. In the painting it was so beautiful; it was fulfilling some purpose, it had some meaning. Now it has no meaning.

Just... you can take one of my eyes out of its socket, and it will be a dead eye, and there will be no meaning in it. Right now if you look into my eyes, there is great meaning — because they exist in my total context; they are part of a poetry, they are part of a bigger painting. Meaning is always in reference to something bigger than you.

The day Nietzsche declared there is no God and God is dead, man fell out of context — HE fell, at least, out of context. Without God man cannot have any significance, because man is a small word in the great epic of God, man is a small note in the great orchestra of God. That small single note will be monotonous; it will be jarring to the ears, it will be maddening.

That's what happened to Nietzsche. He authentically believed in his own statement. He was a believer — a believer who believes in himself. He believed that God is dead AND man is free. But he simply became mad, not free. And this century has followed Friedrich Nietzsche in a thousand and one ways, and the whole century has gone mad. There has never been any other century in world history which was so mad as this century. Future historians will write of it as the age of madness. It is mad — mad because it has lost context.

Why are you alive? For what? You shrug your shoulders. That does not help much. You look accidental. If you were not, there would have been no difference. If you are, there is no difference. You don't make any difference! You are unneeded. You are not fulfilling anything here. Your being or your not being is all the same. How can you feel happy? And how can you remain sane? Accidental? just accidental? Then anything is right — then murder is right! because if everything is accidental, then what does it matter what you do? No action carries any value — then suicide is okay, then murder is okay, then everything is okay!

But everything is not okay, because there are a few things which give you joy and a few things which make you miserable, a few things which create ecstasy and a few things which create only agony, a few things which create only hell and a few things which take you to a world of paradise. No, all things are not the same. But once God is thought to be dead, once you lose contact with the totality — and God is nothing but the totality.... What is a wave when it has forgotten about the ocean? Then it is nothing. It was a great tidal wave when it was part of the ocean.

Remember : the real art arises out of real religion, because religion is finding a communion with reality. Once you are in communion with reality, then real art arises.

You say : I WONDER — WHAT WOULD THE WORLD BE LIKE WITHOUT ART AND THE CREATIVE IMAGINATION THAT MAKES ART POSSIBLE?

If the ninety percent so-called art disappears, the world will be far richer — because then there will be real art. If these mad pretenders go... and I am not saying that they should not paint — they should paint, but as therapy. It IS therapeutic. Picasso needs therapy; he should paint, but those paintings should not be on exhibition — or if they are, then only in madhouses. They may help a few mad people to have a release; they are cathartic.

Real art means something that helps you to be meditative. Gurdjieff used to call real art objective art — that helps you to meditate. The Taj Mahal is real art. Have you gone to the Taj Mahal? It is worth going to. On a full-moon night, just sitting there and looking at that beautiful masterpiece you will be filled with the unknown. You will start feeling something from the beyond.

I would like to tell you the story of how the Taj Mahal came into existence.

A man came from Shiraz, Iran. He was called Shirazi because he had come from Shiraz. He was a GREAT artist, the most famous from Shiraz. And he was a miracle man; a thousand and one stories had come before he came to India. Shah Jehan was the emperor; he heard about those stories. He invited the sculptor to come to the court. And Shirazi was a mystic, a Sufi mystic.

Shah Jehan asked him, "I have heard that you can sculpt the whole body of a man or a woman just by touching his or her hand and not seeing his or her face at all. Is it true?"

Shirazi said, "Give me a chance — but with one condition. Put twenty-five beautiful women from your palace behind a screen, behind a curtain. Let their hands simply be available to me outside the curtain. I will touch their hands and I will choose the person — but with one condition. Whomsoever I choose I will make an image of : if the image comes absolutely true and you are satisfied, your whole court is satisfied, then that woman will be my woman — I want to get married to her, I want a woman from your palace."

Shah Jehan was ready. He said, "That's perfectly okay."

Twenty-five slave girls, beautiful slave girls, were put behind a curtain. He went from the first to the second to the twenty-fifth, rejecting all. Just out of playfulness, Shah Jehan's daughter, just to play a joke, was also standing behind the screen — when twenty-five were rejected, she put out her hand. He touched her hand, closed his eyes, felt something, and said, "This is my hand." And he put a ring on the daughter's hand to signify that "If I succeed, then she is going to be my wife."

The emperor reached behind the screen and he was terrified : "What has this girl done?" But he was not worried because it was almost impossible to make a statue of the whole woman just by touching her hand.

For three months, Shirazi disappeared into a room; day and night he worked. And after three months he asked the emperor and the whole court to come — and the emperor could not believe his eyes. It was exactly the same! He WAS capable. He could not find a single fault; he WANTED to find a fault, because he was not willing that his daughter should be married to a poor man. But now there was no way. He had given his word.

He was so disturbed, and his wife was so much disturbed that his wife fell ill. She was pregnant, and while giving birth to the child, she died — out of agony. Her name was Mumtaz Mahal.

And the king became so desperate : how to save his daughter? He asked the sculptor to come and he told him the whole thing, "It has been a mistake. And the girl is at fault, but look at my situation : my wife has died and the reason is that she could not agree to the idea of her daughter going with a poor man. And I cannot agree either — although I have given you my promise."

The sculptor, the artist, said, "There is no need to be so much worried. You should have told me. I will go back. No need to be worried. I will not ask; I will go back to Shiraz. Forget about it!"

But the king said, "That is not possible; I cannot forget. I have given you a promise, my word. You wait. Let me think."

The prime minister suggested, "You do one thing : your wife

has died and this is a great artist and he has proved himself —
tell him to make a model in the memory of your wife. You should
create a beautiful tomb, the most beautiful in the world. And
make it a condition that if you approve of his model, then you
will have to give your daughter to him in marriage. If you don't
approve, it is finished."

The matter was talked over with the artist and he was willing;
he said, "Perfectly okay."

"Now," the king thought, "I will never approve."

And Shirazi made many models, and they were so beautiful, but
still the king persisted and he said, "No, no, no."

The prime minister became desperate, because those models
were rare. EACH model was rare, and to say no to it was unjust.
HE rumoured around, particularly to the sculptor, "The girl that
you have chosen, the daughter of the king, is very ill." For one
week she was very ill, then the next week she became very very
ill, and the third week she died — in the rumours.

When the rumour reached the sculptor that the girl had died,
he made his last model. The girl was dead. His heart was broken.
And this was going to be the last model. He brought it to the
king and he approved of it. The trick was that the girl was dead
so there was no question of marrying.

That model became the Taj Mahal. That model was created
by a Sufi mystic. How could he create the whole image of the
woman just by touching her hand once? He must have been in
a different kind of space. He must have been in that moment
without mind. That moment must have been a moment of great
meditation. In that moment he touched the energy, and just by
feeling the energy he created the whole shape.

Now this can be understood far more logically because of
Kirlian photography, because each energy has its own pattern.
Your face is not accidental; your face is there because you have
a particular energy pattern. Your eyes, your hair, your colour,
all are there because you have a particular energy pattern.

Meditators have been working on energy patterns down the
ages. Once you know the energy pattern, you know the whole

personality. You know in and out, all — because it is the energy pattern that creates everything. You know past, you know present, you know future. Once the energy pattern has been understood, there is the key, the nucleus, of all that has happened to you and all that is going to happen.

This is objective art. This man created the Taj Mahal.

On a full-moon night, meditating on the Taj Mahal, your heart will throb with new love. The Taj Mahal carries that energy of love still. Mumtaz Mahal died because of her love for the daughter; Shah Jehan suffered because of the love; and this Shirazi created this model because he suffered deeply, he was wounded deeply, because his future was dark. The woman he had chosen was no more. Out of great love and meditativeness the Taj Mahal came into existence. It still carries the vibe. It is not an ordinary monument; it is special. So are the pyramids in Egypt, and there are many many things in the world created as objective art — created by those who knew what they were doing, created by great meditators. So are the Upanishads, so are the sutras of Buddha, so are Jesus' statements.

Remember, to me, creativity means meditativeness, creativity means a state of no-mind — then God descends in you, then love flows out of you. Then something happens out of your well-being, overflowing well-being. It is a blessing. Otherwise it is a vomit.

You can paint, you can write, as a therapy, but burn your paintings and burn your poetry. You need not go on exhibiting your vomit to people.

And the people who become interested in your vomit must be ill themselves; they also need therapy — because if you become interested in something, you show who you are, where you are.

I am all for objective art, I am ALL for a meditative art, I am all for something from God to descend. You become the vehicle.

And you ask : A TOLSTOY COULD NEVER BECOME A BUDDHA.

Who has told you this? A Tolstoy CAN become a Buddha, WILL become a Buddha sooner or later.

And you say :... BUT THEN COULD A BUDDHA WRITE *War and Peace?*

And what has Buddha been doing? What am I doing here? Have you read Krishna's Gita? — it is *War and Peace*! Tolstoy could write *War and Peace, Anna Karenina* and many other beautiful things, not because he was Tolstoy but in spite of being a Tolstoy.

Dostoyevsky has written *The Idiot, Crime and Punishment,* and, one of the most beautiful things, *The Brothers Karamazov* — not because he was Dostoyevsky but in spite of it. Something of him was that of a Buddha; something of him was immensely religious. Dostoyevsky was a religious man — not totally, but a part, a fragment of him, was immensely religious. That's why *The Brothers Karamazov* has such a beautiful quality in it. It is not just out of an ordinary man; something has come from the divine. Dostoyevsky has been taken possession of by the God, he has become a vehicle. Of course, he is not a perfect vehicle, so many things go on from HIS mind. Still, *The Brothers Karamazov* is beautiful. If there had been no Dostoyevsky, no memory, no ego, no pathology, then *The Brothers Karamazov* would have been another New Testament; it would have been the same as Jesus' statements or a Diamond Sutra or an Upanishad. He has the quality!

The second question :

It keeps occurring to me that it is incredibly easy for all my rubbish to just fall away and disappear — that I could just choose to be delighted all the time right now. Am I kidding myself? Is it really that easy? That's ridiculous.

VANDANA, IT IS RIDICULOUS, BUT STILL IT HAPPENS, It is unbelievable, but it is true. Truth is always unbelievable because truth is a mystery. That which YOU can believe, cannot be true. Just because YOU can believe, it can't be true. All that you can believe must be a lie. You ARE a lie; you can believe only in lie. Truth is too much — it looks ridiculous, it looks absurd, because it is paradoxical and illogical. Yes, it is so.

You say : IT KEEPS OCCURRING TO ME THAT IT IS INCREDIBLY EASY FOR ALL MY RUBBISH TO JUST FALL AWAY AND DISAPPEAR...

Yes, it is so, Vandana. It is absolutely easy. In fact, you need not drop it even. Just don't go on holding it, that's all. It is like a fist — I can go on keeping my fist closed, I am putting effort in closing it. But if I drop that effort, if I don't close it, the fist opens of its own accord. Not that I open it — I close it, but I don't open it. Once I stop closing it, it opens of its own accord.

Truth is your nature, God is your nature. It can happen right now — you are just not to prevent it. You cannot manage to make it happen, but you can go on preventing it for lives together. That's what you have been doing.

It is unbelievable, it is incredible, it doesn't seem that it is possible. You cannot believe it that you yourself are preventing your bliss, that you yourself are destroying your paradise, that you yourself are the problem. That hurts, that idea hurts. You say, "No, it can't be so. There must be some cause which is beyond me." Then you feel good because then the responsibility is no more on you. You have to find some scapegoat to keep your ego intact. It is because of your past karmas that you are suffering — then it is perfectly okay; you have found a rational explanation. Or it is because you are punished for Adam and Eve's sin — then you have found a rationalization. Or maybe there is no God and you are just accidental, so one has to suffer — you have found an explanation.

Your so-called philosophies and religions are nothing but explanations which keep you miserable. They are tricks just to save your face. I would like you to be reminded again and again that it is YOU and you alone and nobody else. The moment you recognize it, the moment you allow this insight to penetrate your whole being the fist will open of its own accord.

You say, Vandana, IT KEEPS OCCURRING TO ME THAT IT IS INCREDIBLY EASY...

Yes, it is incredibly easy. Even to say 'easy' is not right, because 'easy' also means a little bit difficult, something of the difficult still remains in it. Because easy is not very difficult, not so difficult, but something of the difficulty hangs around it. It is NOT even easy, because it is not difficult at all. It is NOT even close, because it is NOT far at all. It is within you, it is you, it has already happened.

IT KEEPS OCCURRING TO ME THAT IT IS INCREDIBLY EASY FOR ALL MY RUBBISH TO JUST FALL AWAY AND DISAPPEAR — THAT I COULD JUST CHOOSE TO BE DELIGHTED ALL THE TIME RIGHT NOW.

Yes, it is your choice.
AM I KIDDING MYSELF?
No, not at all.
IS IT REALLY THAT EASY?
Yes. A story for you, Vandana.

A man went to a prostitute and asked if she could do something special for him. She agreed for an extra fifty pounds. "Right," he said. "Put on this raincoat and these rubber boots and put up this umbrella."

"Strange," thought the prostitute, but she did as he asked.

"Now," he said, "get up on the table and bang this drum like thunder, at the same time switching the light on and off like lightning."

Again she did as he asked. Then he got a bucket of water and started pouring it over both their heads.

This continued for four hours until, soaking wet and tired, the prostitute said, "Enough! Enough! I know fifty quid is fifty quid, but don't you ever want to make love to me?"

"What?" exclaimed the man. "In weather like this? You must be crazy!"

The weather is created by you. You can stop it ANY moment.

And the last question :

Why do I go on misunderstanding you?

BECAUSE YOU ARE NOT CONSCIOUS. It is natural in an unconscious state. Rather than trying to understand me, start becoming more conscious.

And you cannot simply understand me and remain unconscious the remaining time; it can't happen that way. You will have to bring the quality of consciousness to your twenty-four-hour life. You cannot just be conscious listening in the morning — and then you fall asleep. That is not possible. Consciousness is a continuum — if you are asleep twenty-three hours, you will be asleep here too. You can be asleep with open eyes.

You will have to bring more and more consciousness —not only while you are listening to me. Walking, be more conscious. Talking, be more conscious. Even listening to your wife, be more conscious! Who listens to his own wife? She goes on saying things and you know what she is saying, you have heard them so many times. Who listens to her own husband? Who listens? People go on talking — who bothers?

Listen even when the dog is barking. Listen attentively. Only then will you be able to listen to me too. Listen attentively when there is a traffic noise. Don't close yourself to it — you tend to. And the only way to close yourself is to become unconscious. There is no other way. You can put off your consciousness — then the traffic goes on roaring and you need not be disturbed. You become insensitive to it. The train passes by and you are insensitive. The plane is passing and you are insensitive. That's how you have become.

Scientists say we are only two percent alert; ninety-eight percent we are insensitive. We are afraid. There are so many things happening — if all those things become available we will go mad.

Become more sensitive. You will not go mad. Closing yourself to life you have become mad. Open up, listen to everything.

Noise also has to be listened to as you listen to music. And if you listen attentively you will be surprised — noise is music. And if you don't listen attentively, music is noise. If you listen attentively, the barking dog is a Buddha-sermon. If you don't listen attentively, when Buddha is speaking only a dog is barking.

You try to understand me; you make all the effort, I know, but that is not going to help. You will have to bring awareness from as many doors as possible. Eating, smell the food. Let your nose become alive again — it has been dead. Man has completely lost his nose, his smelling capacity. While eating food, taste with great awareness. Food is God. It is nourishment, something of God is in it — otherwise how will it nourish you? Something of life is in it. Packaged life, packaged sun, is in it. That's what the trees are doing continuously — you cannot absorb the sun directly, they do the job for you. They absorb the sun and then you eat the apple — the apple is packaged sun, ready for you.

In the future there is a possibility... and I would like it to happen — because only then can poverty disappear from the world, and starvation and hunger. If trees can do it, why cannot man do it directly? Everybody just has to wear a cap, a special cap made to absorb the sun directly. And it can be automatic too — whenever you are hungry it will absorb, and whenever you are not hungry it will not absorb. If trees can do it — that they can transform sun into food — why not you? Man has not looked into these possibilities, because man's whole mind is concerned with war. Man has created the atom bomb and the hydrogen bomb — why can't man make small things like these which can change the whole earth? And once you have a special arrangement for absorbing food direct from the sun, all the problems will disappear — because ninety percent of illnesses come from the stomach.

And this continuous inequality in the world — that a few people have more than they need and a few people don't have what they need — it can be dropped. Sooner or later it is going to happen. It has to happen, otherwise the earth cannot be saved.

When you are eating an apple, remember, be grateful to the

tree. It has done something for you that you cannot do on your own. Be grateful to the sun — you are eating the sun, you are eating energy. Taste it, smell it, touch it, be sensitive to it, be open to it, and you will find windows opening in you. Taking a bath, be open to it. Eighty percent of your body is water — be thankful, enjoy this shower, this water falling on you. Let your inside water be thrilled.

Become more and more aware and conscious of whatsoever you are doing, and then you will be able to understand me more and more. Right now you are in a drunken state.

A small story to meditate...

It happened in Africa. A political rebel had been condemned to death. However, the sultan was in an indulgent frame of mind. When the prisoner was brought before him, his majesty declared : "I'm going to give you a chance for your life. Before us there stand three tents. In each tent there is an almost superhuman task to perform. If you succeed in all the three tents, I will pardon you.

"In the first tent is a gallon of wine : you must drink it all down within fifteen minutes. In the second tent is a ferocious tiger suffering from a horrible toothache : you must extract the tooth in fifteen minutes. In the third tent there is a powerfully built Amazonian virgin who has resisted the advances of the strongest men in my realm. You cannot overpower her, but you have fifteen minutes to seduce her."

The prisoner thanked the sultan for being given a chance to live, and then proceeded to the first tent. In ten minutes he emerged staggeringly drunk, holding upside-down an empty wine jug in one hand. On unsteady feet he plunged into the second tent. Seconds later, everyone's blood curdled because of the terrible screams and roars which came forth from that tent. About eight minutes later, the prisoner emerged from the second tent, a horrible bloody mess, covered with long scratches, deep bites and fearful gouges from the tiger's claws. To look at him was sickening.

Reeling up to one of the royal attendants, the prisoner demanded : "Now where is the girl with the toothache?"

CHAPTER
8

The Tender Trap

The first question :

If truth cannot be expressed in words, then why have all the Buddhas used words?

A parable :

*T*HE GREAT MYSTIC, Rabia of Basra, was immensely beautiful. And a beauty not of this world. Once a rich young man from Iran comes to Basra. He asks people, "Is there anything that is out of the way, something special here?"

"Yes," they all tell him. "We have the most beautiful woman of the world!"

The young man naturally becomes interested and he asks, "Where can I find her?"

And they all laugh and say, "Well, where else?... in a brothel!"

That repulses the rich young man, but finally he decides to go. And when he gets there, the matron asks for an exorbitant fee. He pays the fee and is ushered in. There, in a silent and simple room, a figure is praying. What beauty she has! He has never seen such beauty and grace, not even in his dreams. Just to be there is a benediction, and the prayerful atmosphere starts affecting him. He forgets about his passion. He is entering into another kind of space. He is drugged. He is turned on to God.

An hour passes and he intensely feels he is in a temple! Oh, such joy and such purity! He goes on feasting on her beauty. But it is no more the beauty of a human being — it is God's beauty. It no more has anything to do with the body — it is utterly other-worldly.

And then Rabia opens her eyes, those lotus eyes, and he looks into them, and there is no woman in front of him — he is facing God. And this way the whole night passes, as if it were only a moment.

The sun is rising and its rays are coming through the windows, and he feels it is time to go. He says to Rabia, "I am your slave. Tell me anything, anything in the world that I can do for you."

She says, "I have only one little request."

He asks, "What is it?"

Rabia says, "Never tell anybody what you have seen and experienced here. Allow the people to come to me — this beauty is nothing but a trap set for them. I use it as a door for them to enter God. Please, promise me that you will never tell others what you have experienced here tonight. Let them come to a whore and a brothel, because otherwise they will never come to me."

"Oh!" he says, "So this is the secret of this city. The whole city clamours after your beauty, yet nobody tells me about his experience."

Rabia laughs and says, "Yes, I extract the promise, this promise, from all of them."

Rabia used her beauty as a trap. Buddha used his words as a trap. Krishna used his flute as a trap. Meera used her dance as a trap.

You have to be trapped. And you can only be trapped in ways that you CAN understand. You have to be taken from the known into the unknown, but the beginning has to be in the known.

You understand passion. The young man was not in search of God, but he became interested in a beautiful body, in a beautiful woman — and was trapped. He had gone there because of his passion. Once he was there in the presence of Rabia, the passion started changing — it became prayer.

You can understand words, that's why all the Buddhas have used words, knowing perfectly well, saying again and again, that the truth cannot be expressed in words. But you understand words and the truth cannot be expressed in words, then how to communicate? The journey has to start from where you are. The Buddhas have to speak words. Words will bring you closer to the Buddhas; words will not give you truth, but they will bring you closer to the Buddhas. Once you are close to them, you will start forgetting the words; you will start falling into silence.

The words cannot express truth, but they can bring you close to a Buddha. And that is more than you can expect of poor words! That's why Buddhas go on saying on the one hand words are meaningless, on the other hand they go on using words.

They ARE meaningful for you — you don't know the language of silence, you don't know the language of being. You know only your mind; you have forgotten all else. If I am to bring you out of your mind, I will have to start from the mind, I will have to take your mind in confidence — then only the pilgrimage towards no-mind.....

The second question :

You have spoken about art. You have said that most of it is ill, that Picasso's paintings are only mad and a therapy for him. I agree with you — but I also know that I love the aesthetics of decadence. I know too that it is my mirror of my illness — but I too believe that there exists a little more as well.

This little difference is important. In the little difference, life is hidden. I loved you speaking about aesthetics. Don't you think there is a beauty in the leaves of autumn? Don't you think there can also be an acceptance of madness? a surrender and knowing that all is good? The setting sun — what colours! Don't you think there exists a glimpse of the unknown in the paintings of Picasso? Don't you think there exists a madness without consciousness and a madness with consciousness?

In real beauty I find always life and death. For me this problem is not abstract — I live it. I love a dying violet.

The question is from Prem Ashok.

IT IS SIGNIFICANT to go into the aesthetics of life.

First thing : while listening to me, remember you are neither to agree with me nor to disagree with me. If you agree or disagree, you miss the point. Agreement, disagreement, is of the mind. When you say you agree with me, what are you saying? You are really saying, "I agree with you." You are saying, "Whatsoever you are saying is in tune with my own thinking." But if this is agreement, then I will not be able to transform you.

If you disagree with me, that is also the same : something is going against your prejudice, your idea, then you disagree. When something goes with your idea, you agree; when something goes against your idea, you disagree — but you remain there, agreeing, disagreeing. And in both ways, you will not be able to understand what I am making available to you.

You, please, forget about agreeing, disagreeing — this is not a philosophical discourse. I am not teaching you philosophy or aesthetics. I am simply opening my heart to you. You just listen! Don't be in a hurry to agree or disagree; don't go on agreeing, disagreeing while I am speaking to you; otherwise, your agreements, disagreements will become a barrier.

First listen. First get in tune with me! First fall in harmony with me. Let there arise an accord. Accord does not mean agreement. Accord simply means you are in love with me — not with what I say. You are simply in love with my being. My saying this or that is irrelevant.

First you fall in accord with me... and from THERE insights will start exploding in you. They will be transforming.

You say : YOU HAVE SPOKEN ABOUT ART. YOU HAVE SAID THAT MOST OF IT IS ILL, THAT PICASSO'S PAINTINGS ARE ONLY MAD AND A THERAPY FOR HIM. I AGREE WITH YOU...

You miss the point. It was not a statement to be agreed with or disagreed with. I was opening a door. I was not saying anything about Picasso; I was just illustrating a point; I was just giving you an example so that things could become more concrete. I was not condemning Picasso!

You say you agree with me? That means these were your ideas before you heard me, and you jumped upon them. You said, "Right! Osho, you are right because YOU agree with me. You must be right."

If you feel that way, you have protected yourself. You will remain the same; in fact, you have become more strong, you have strengthened yourself. Can't you avoid agreement, disagreement? It is difficult, because the mind is so accustomed to agreeing, disagreeing — immediately.

The moment you hear something, either you say yes or you say no. Can't you avoid saying yes and no? Can't you simply listen? There is no hurry to say yes or no. Let the thing SOAK into your being. Drink it! Let it move into your bloodstream. Let it go into your very marrow. From THERE something will arise, sprout — and that will be new

And for that new I am working here. Whatsoever I say is only a device. It has nothing absolute about it; it is arbitrary. And that's why with the agreement there is disagreement too.

You say : I AGREE WITH YOU — BUT I ALSO KNOW THAT I LOVE THE AESTHETICS OF DECADENCE.

The mind is very clever and diplomatic. It says : "On one point I agree with you; on another point I don't." But you remain the same! You have not changed a little bit. You have not even taken a single step towards me.

I KNOW TOO THAT IT IS MY MIRROR OF MY ILLNESS — BUT...

And remember, those 'buts' are very very significant : those 'buts' are your diplomatic strategies. You are only half-heartedly saying :

I KNOW THAT IT IS MY MIRROR OF MY ILLNESS BUT I TOO BELIEVE THAT THERE EXISTS A LITTLE MORE AS WELL.

No, there exists nothing more.

THIS LITTLE DIFFERENCE IS IMPORTANT, YOU SAY. IN THE LITTLE DIFFERENCE LIFE IS HIDDEN. I LOVED YOU SPEAKING

ABOUT AESTHETICS. DON'T YOU THINK THERE IS A BEAUTY IN THE LEAVES OF AUTUMN?

Yes, there is beauty in the leaves of autumn — but those leaves don't know that they are dying; those leaves don't know that they are decadent. Those leaves are STILL living! They have NO fear of death. Those leaves are living their autumn! They have lived their spring, now they are living their autumn. Those leaves have lived their life, now they are living their death. And there is a great difference.

When you see autumn leaves, the idea of death arises in you, not in the leaves. The leaves are uncorrupted by any idea. They are in total suchness. Spring was good, so is autumn. And life was beautiful — those green days and the winds and the clouds... they were beautiful and so are these days! Leaves are drying and becoming pale and falling to the ground — and they are enjoying! because they are going back to the source. It is from where they had come in the first place. They were born out of the earth, they played in the winds, they rose high in the sky, they had their day — now they are tired, now they want to be rejuvenated, they want to fall back into the womb. They are perfectly happy! There is no hitch, no complaint, no grudge, there is no fear, no apprehension.

Autumn leaves are not decadent. Nature knows NO decadence! Nature is ALWAYS alive, even in death. Nature knows no death. Death is a human invention. And why does man have to invent death? — because man has invented the ego. Death is a by-product of the ego. The MOMENT you say "I am," death has entered. The leaves have never said that they are — death cannot enter.

If you don't say "I am," how can you die? To die, first you have to be.

Just meditate over it. Don't agree and disagree with me! just meditate over it. If you DON'T say 'I', then where is the problem? You are not there. There is eternal silence... absolute emptiness, what Buddha calls SHUNYATA. Now, who is there to die? From where is decadence possible now?

That's why I repeat again : nature knows no death — because in death also there is life. Death is a phase of life, an inactive phase of life is death, a silent phase of life. Death is life relaxing. Death is life gone to sleep, to rest. Death is a pause — to rejuvenate oneself. Death is a cleansing. Death is a process of destroying the unnecessary and the unessential that gathers around oneself in the process of life. Death is an unburdening.

But, if you don't burden yourself, there is no death. If you unburden yourself, then there is no death. If you don't have the idea that "I am separate from existence," how can you think that "I will die"? In the separation, behind the separation, comes the shadow of death.

Those leaves have never thought they are separate, so don't impose your ideas upon the autumn leaves. That is not fair.

You say : DON'T YOU THINK THERE IS A BEAUTY IN THE LEAVES OF AUTUMN?

There IS beauty! because there is no decadence. There IS beauty because there is no death. There IS beauty, because there is eternity.

DON'T YOU THINK THERE CAN ALSO BE AN ACCEPTANCE OF MADNESS?

I KNOW THERE CAN BE AN ACCEPTANCE OF MADNESS — but the moment you accept madness, you are no more mad. Madness exists only in its rejection. Have you ever found any madman who agrees that he is mad? Then go to a madhouse and ask all the mad people who are there — nobody will accept that he is mad. And if somebody accepts that he is mad, that means he is no more mad. How can madness accept? Only wisdom can accept.

In accepting madness, the quality, the very quality of madness is transformed. You have brought a light and the darkness disappears.

Remember : madness exists only in rejection, and the more you reject, the more you will be mad. The foolish man goes on rejecting his foolishness, and becomes more of a fool. The ugly man goes on rejecting his ugliness and becomes uglier. And the madman goes on rejecting his madness, and becomes more and more mad.

Accept... and ugliness disappears, grace arises. Accept... and sin is transformed into saintliness. Accept... and madness is no more madness.

Acceptance is the alchemical process of transforming everything. Whatsoever is, accept it. From where does the rejection come? The rejection comes because of some idea in you of how things should be. You cannot accept your foolishness because you have this idea that you should be wise. You cannot accept your madness because you have this idea that you should be sane. You cannot accept anything because you have the opposite idea.

In acceptance, all ideals have to be dropped. When you are not searching for wisdom, only then can you accept your foolishness. But in accepting foolishness, one becomes wise.

This is the secret. In accepting your ugliness, beauty arises. That's why you don't see an ugly tree, and you don't see an ugly animal, and you don't see an ugly bird. Why? Because there is no rejection. There is great acceptance. They live in suchness — tathata. Whosoever they are and whatsoever they are, they don't hanker for something else, they don't hanker to be otherwise — they are in tune with themselves. In that very harmoniousness is grace. Grace is a quality that comes when you accept life as it is — and grace is beauty.

I know madness can be accepted, but mad people don't accept it. If they accept, they will become enlightened.

Have you accepted things that you find in yourself? or do you go on rejecting them? do you go on hiding them? do you go on covering them? do you pretend to be somebody else that you are not? Have you accepted yourself as you are? Are you ready to expose yourself as you are? in your utter nudity? If you are not ready then you are also mad. Sooner or later you will accumulate so much rejection and so much madness that you will not be able to control it.

Civilization drives people mad because civilization forces

ideals on people's minds. Man is the only animal on earth who goes mad, because only man has perfectionist ideas. A dog is simply a dog; and perfectly happy with being a dog. And no dog is trying to become a super-dog. But man, EVERY man, is trying to become a superman hence the madness.

And you say :... A SURRENDER AND KNOWING THAT ALL IS GOOD?

When you say "all is good," all is not good, something is wrong. This is again covering. When you say "all is good," it is a consolation. If all is good, there is no need to say anything a,out it. If all is good, all IS good — saying betrays you. You only say all is good when you know that all is not good.

Whom are you trying to befool? You are trying to befool yourself. You are trying to create a kind of auto-hypnosis by saying all is good. You are following Emile Coué. You know you are ill, but you go on saying, "I am not ill. Who says I am ill? I am perfectly happy and perfectly okay." And you know all the time. In fact, because you know you are ill, that's why you are repeating this.

Coue was teaching — he had a great following once — to go on repeating, "Every day, in every way, I am getting better and better. I am healthy, I am wise, I am beautiful." But when you say "I am wise," what exactly are you saying? If you ARE wise, then what is the point? Deep down you know you are not. Because you know you are not, you are trying to become wise by saying it, by imposing it.

When somebody says, "All is good," look into his eyes and you will find something is gnawing his heart, something is disturbing him. He does not want to get disturbed; he wants to pretend all is good. These pretensions won't help.

All is CERTAINLY good! but there is no need to say it.

Lao Tzu has said : There was a time when people were religious, but then there was no religion. Then came religion, and people became irreligious.

A strange statement, but of great significance and of great

profundity, and great truth is contained in it. When people are moral, they are oblivious of the fact. When people are really healthy, they are not aware of it. Have you not watched it, healthy people? Healthy people are NOT aware of it. Healthy people don't read literature on naturopathy. Healthy people are simply oblivious of the body.

In the ancient Indian scriptures, health is defined as 'bodilessness'. I have never come across a better definition. One should be unaware of the body, then one is healthy. But you go on thinking about your illnesses, and you go on reading about health, nature foods, naturopathy — and there are a thousand and one fads around the world. And the more you read these things, the more ill you will be, and the more unnatural you will be, because the more conscious you will become.

I have seen people who are in search of health — they are continuously conscious of it. Just a little movement of the wind in their stomachs and they are there. Just a little heaviness in the head and they are there. Just a little pain somewhere and they are there. Now, the body is a complex and big mechanism; a thousand and one things are going on. If you are continuously looking inside you will go mad.

Just try it for twenty-four hours, just go on looking inside at what is happening there — blood is circulating or not? the intestine is working or not? the stomach is digesting or not? Just look inside your body, and within twenty-four hours you will be as ill as one can be. Twenty-four hours' work, and you will be on the bed....

The body, when healthy, remains in darkness. There is no need even to think about it. Healthy roots remain underneath the earth in darkness. All that is healthy remains unaware.

In Sanskrit, we have a word VEDANA. It has two meanings, very strange meanings; one meaning is knowledge, the other meaning is suffering. Knowledge is suffering. One word has two meanings : knowledge and suffering. You know only when you suffer. You know about your head only when there is a headache. When the headache is gone, the head too is gone.

Now, Ashok, you say: DON'T YOU THINK THERE CAN ALSO BE AN ACCEPTANCE OF MADNESS? A SURRENDER AND KNOWING THAT ALL IS GOOD?

Yes, there is, but it is not a consolation. It is not even a statement. One lives in it. It is an existential experience.

But I would like you to remember that Picasso had not accepted his madness. If he had accepted it, his paintings would have changed. If he had accepted it, he would have become a Buddha. Nietzsche did not accept his madness. If he had accepted there would have been a great change, mutation; he would not have died mad.

Van Gogh did not accept his madness; if he HAD accepted he would not have committed suicide. Now, Van Gogh committing suicide at the age of thirty-three, so young... life was still ahead. And Van Gogh committing suicide simply shows what kind of paintings he was doing — they are suicidal. Before he committed suicide he became mad; for one year he was continuously mad. In fact, his best paintings are those that he painted in his madness. They ARE bizarre, they are overflowing neurosis; they depict, they mirror a madman's mind. He painted even that day when he committed suicide; even in that painting there is the shadow of suicide. He must have been brooding, he must have been thinking... he was continuously thinking about suicide! He had not even accepted life — how could he accept death? But he was a genius; about that there is no doubt.

Picasso is a genius. But to be a genius is not necessarily to be a wise man. A genius can be mad. A genius can be a wise man. Buddha is also a genius, but one who has awakened to his innermost core. Van Gogh is also a genius, but lives in absolute mechanicalness. Even without being sane he has painted so beautifully — had he been sane, you can imagine what his creation would have been. That would have been a great gift to the world. The world has missed something beautiful.

You say: THE SETTING SUN — WHAT COLOURS!

But do you know? The sun never sets. It is only setting for

you. It is rising somewhere else. The sun knows NO setting. It is always rising, it is continuously rising — each moment is a new birth. For you, it looks like the sun is setting; but for the sun, it is always rising and rising and rising. It is eternal rising.

And so is the vision of an enlightened man. Life knows no death. Life has never known death. The sun never sets. Even if this sun dies, it will be born somewhere else again. Every star melts as surely as every snowflake, only to be born in another time, another place. Nothing ever dies. Death is improbable, impossible. Death exists not.

It is in your mind, Ashok. The sunset is beautiful — because it is another rise, it is another kind of morning. Have you not seen old trees, how beautiful they are? — because they don't know of oldness. In their ancientness, they have such beauty. It rarely happens with man that an old man is beautiful, but whenever it happens you can be certain that man has lived his life to the full.

A Rabindranath becomes more and more beautiful as he become old, as his hair starts turning grey and white, as his body starts turning older and older. He attains to a new quality of beauty — which no young man can have. Youth has its own beauty, but it is shallow; it can't have depth. It is more of the physical and less of the spiritual. It is more of the body; it can't have much profundity.

Youth has not lived yet to be so profound. An old man, a Rabindranath, who has lived life — its joys, its sadnesses, its blessings, its curses, its days, its dark nights — who has seen life in its variety and richness, who has suffered and who has been blessed, naturally becomes profound, naturally gains depth. In his old age, you can see a kind of luminosity, something like a flame inside, very deep, filtering through; the rays come outside too. With his white hair and old age, he looks like Everest — that white hair has become like ancient virgin snow on the Himalayan peak.

If a man lives his life totally, is not afraid to live, he will become every day more and more beautiful.

The child has a kind of beauty, youth has another kind of beauty, old age has another kind of beauty — and death is also beautiful. But ONLY if you have lived, otherwise death is very ugly — because life has been ugly, how can death be beautiful? Death is simply the last statement, the testament : your whole life is condensed in that last statement.

A man who has not lived rightly, or who has lived half-heartedly, will not be able to relax in death — he will cling to life. He will shout deep in his heart, "Give me a little time more! Don't take me away — I have not lived yet! I am not yet ripe! I have missed opportunities. A little more opportunity I need." There will be great longing and there will be great sadness. The man is not ripe. He will hold on to the shore : he will try hard to be here. He will cling, and that clinging will create his ugliness.

When a man has lived, loved, meditated, danced, prayed, and has done all kinds of things, whatsoever... has moved in all kinds of desires, has not left anything unexperienced; has lived in sin and sainthood, has gone to the deepest darkness and has arisen to the highest sunlit peak, has moved freely and wildly... a man whose whole commitment was with life and there was NO other commitment; a man who has not sacrificed his life for some stupid idea : God, heaven, motherland, religion, politics, communism, socialism; a man who has not sacrificed his life for anything... because life is so valuable that it cannot be sacrificed for anything else. Everything else can be sacrificed to life — life to none. Life is God! A man who has lived life with reverence, with totality, will be able to relax. When death comes he will simply relax, as the child relaxes in his mother's lap. He will close his eyes, he will say goodbye — his statement will be that of fulfillment, gratitude. There will be a prayer on his lips that "I am thankful. All that happened was incredible. I was not worthy of it, but you made me worthy. I had not earned it, but you went on pouring your grace. I cannot pay it back." He will die in deep gratitude, and there will be grace and there will be joy. And there will be that luminosity which always comes with fulfillment. He is dying a ripe man, mature, wise. Life has made him wise.

But... this is not the setting of a sun. He is simply going into rest, will rise again. Every star melts as surely as every snowflake, only to be born in another time, another place.

You say : THE SETTING SUN — WHAT COLOURS! DON'T YOU THINK THERE EXISTS A GLIMPSE OF THE UNKNOWN IN THE PAINTINGS OF PICASSO?

Yes, it is there, but it is a very perverted glimpse. It is there! distorted — because Picasso's mirror is distorted. It is like a mirror broken in a thousand pieces and you have somehow put it together, and it reflects — that reflection is a distorted reflection.

Buddha is one piece. He also reflects the same reality, but because he is one piece, he is no more in fragments, he is integrated, he has become a silent pool of energy, a reservoir with no ripples, with no thoughts, with NO madness... because mind is madness. And Buddha exists without mind — there is no possibility of any madness. Only the mind can go mad!

It is the SAME reality that is reflected in a madman and in a wise man, but the difference is in the mirrors, not in the reality. When I see the trees and you see the trees, the trees are the same — but there is a great difference. If your mirror is broken, if your mirror is covered with dust, layers of dust, of ancient dust of many many lives, your reflection cannot be true to reality, it cannot be of suchness.

Yes, there is a glimpse, EVEN in Picasso, but that glimpse could have been far truer to reality. If Picasso had known something of meditation, if he had known how to drop his continuous thought process, how to drop his mind... the West has forgotten the ways.

And you say : DON'T YOU THINK THERE EXISTS A MADNESS WITHOUT CONSCIOUSNESS AND A MADNESS WITH CONSCIOUSNESS?

I have never heard of a madness with consciousness. All madness is without consciousness. To be conscious and mad is impossible. It is as impossible as it is to have light in the room and darkness too. When the room is lighted, you cannot bring darkness in the room. When you bring light in, darkness is no more.

So is consciousness — consciousness is light, it is a flame, it is a fire. Madness is like darkness. It exists only in an unconscious being.

That's why I say if Picasso had known something of meditation, he would have been benefited immensely and the world would have been benefited immensely too. His creation would have been a great blessing. Right now, as it is, it is simply a statement of madness and nothing else.

And, finally, you say : IN REAL BEAUTY I FIND ALWAYS LIFE AND DEATH.

In real beauty there is neither life nor death — there is eternity. Life and death are our ideas. We go on imposing.... If man disappears from the earth, life and death will both disappear. Trees will live and die, but there will be no life and no death. Birds will sing and one day fall and disappear — there will be life and death, but no idea of life and death. Ideas are all man-made.

And beauty is only when you have pushed aside all man-made ideas. Beauty is eternal — it is beyond life and death. Truth is eternal; it is beyond life and death. Beauty is truth : truth is beauty.

IN REAL BEAUTY I FIND ALWAYS LIFE AND DEATH.

And what do you mean by 'real beauty'? Have you ever seen unreal beauty too? BEAUTY IS REALITY!

There is no unreal beauty. But we go on making distinctions because the mind cannot allow you to see the distinctionless. Everywhere it will make distinctions — real and unreal, good and bad, moral and immoral, holy and unholy, material and spiritual. The mind goes on making distinctions because the mind cannot see the distinctionless —and that which is is distinctionless.

FOR ME THIS PROBLEM IS NOT ABSTRACT — I LIVE IT.

Nobody can live a problem! And if you live a problem, you will be mad. You can live a mystery, not a problem. A problem necessarily goads you for its solution. What is a problem? A problem is something that you cannot leave as it is; it has to be solved. You cannot live a problem! And the problem will not allow you to LIVE at all, unless you solve it. And you have so many problems, and they all clamour for their solution, and they all destroy your life.

Mysteries can be lived. What is the difference between a mystery and a problem? A problem can be solved, a mystery cannot be solved, a mystery is insoluble. A mystery is not a question, and there is no answer for it. You have simply to live it. You have to trust it.

Mind creates problems out of the mystery because the mind cannot trust. Mind is doubt. It goes on putting 'why?' — it goes on creating the question mark everywhere.

Why is the rose beautiful? Now it has become a problem; it has to be solved — why? Some answer has to be found. The beauty of the rose is a mystery — there is no answer. It is simply there. There is no why to it. So is love. So are people. So is music. So is silence. So are the stars and the seas and the mountains... so is this whole.

If you make problems out of it, you will create philosophy. If you don't make any problem out of existence, religion is born in you. Religion knows no problems and no answers. Religion lives life like a child — in absolute awe, wonder, in reverence. In fact, to ask a question is to be irreverent. The question is the beginning of the murder of the mystery. The question is the beginning of demystification.

That's what science has been continuously doing — demystifying. It cannot succeed! It has failed utterly, but it goes on trying. The more it fails, the more madly it tries. The whole effort behind science is : how to demystify existence; how to know every answer for every question — how to make man knowledgeable. If science succeeds, then there will come one day when all questions have been answered. Just think of it! Beyond that will be sheer boredom.

Just think of it! — a day when all questions have been solved, mysteries dissolved, you know every answer. You can go and consult a computer or an encyclopedia; or you can ask the expert but ALL questions are solved, there are no more questions left. That will be the day of utter doom. There will be sheer boredom beyond that. Then there cannot be any joy.

Knowledge kills joy — knowledge is a killjoy. Religion does not trust in knowledge. Religion trusts in ignorance — because ignorance is innocent.

You say : FOR ME THIS PROBLEM IS NOT ABSTRACT...

Problems as such are always abstract. You cannot live a problem : you can live only a mystery. But for that you will have to drop all problems.

I LOVE A DYING VIOLET.

But why? Why can't you love just a violet? Why does it need to die? Why can't you just love a violet? Why 'dying'? Somehow you must be suicidal. Somehow you are death-oriented. Somehow you are destructive. Somehow you enjoy only sadness.

And again, let me repeat : the violet is not dying; the violet is only reborn. It is only in your mind that the violet is dying. But you enjoy death. There is something obsessive in you. It may be just because you are incapable of enjoying life — you have created a substitute : you enjoy death.

I am NOT against enjoying death, but I would like to say to you : if you CANNOT enjoy life, you cannot enjoy death — because death is the culmination, death is the crescendo. Death is the LAST touch, the finishing touch.... Death is not against life : it is life's greatest peak.

The third question :

How to know when it is appropriate to end a love relationship? How can one go deep with a person when he is afraid?

MANTRA, RELATIONSHIP AND LOVE ARE TOTALLY different things. Love is never a relationship, and relationship is never love. Love relates, but it is not a relationship. Relationship is a dead thing, a closed thing. Love is a flowing.

You ask me : HOW TO KNOW WHEN IT IS APPROPRIATE TO END A LOVE RELATIONSHIP?

So the first thing to be reminded of : love is never a relationship. Then something else is masquerading as love. Maybe you are searching for a husband or a wife — you are searching for some security, you are searching for some structure. A structured life is a murdered life.

There is a fixation in the human mind for structures, because in a structured life one feels secure, one knows where one is, one knows where one stands in relationship to the other. It seems that because man is born in the womb of the mother and for nine months remains in a structure, that continues deep down in the psyche — and man is always trying to find a structure somewhere.

If he loves, he wants to make a relationship out of it immediately! He wants to get married. He wants to create a certain conditioning. He wants to make it a contract. Or he enters a church, or he enters a political party, or he enters into ANY club — and he wants to be structured, he wants to know where he stands in the hierarchy, in what relationship. He wants to have an identity — that "I am this." He does not want to remain uncertain.

And life is uncertain. Only death is certain.

Remember : in your whole life, once you have taken birth, only death is certain and everything else is uncertain. Uncertainty is the very core of life. Insecurity is its very spirit.

But we are always hankering for a structure.

Relationship is a structure, and love is unstructured. So love relates, certainly, but never becomes a relationship. Love is a moment-to-moment process. Remember it. Love is a state of your being, not a relationship. There are loving people and there are unloving people. Unloving people pretend to be loving through the relationship. Loving people need not have any relationship — love is enough.

Be a loving person rather than in a love relationship — because relationships happen one day and disappear another day. They are flowers; in the morning they bloom, by the evening they are gone.

You be a loving person, Mantra.

But people find it very difficult to be a loving person, so they create a relationship — and befool that way that "Now I am a loving person because I am in a relationship." And the relationship may be just one of monopoly, possessiveness, exclusiveness. Relationship may be just out of fear, may not have anything to do with love. Relationship may be just a kind of security — financial or something else. The relationship is needed only because love is not there. Relationship is a substitute.

Become alert! Relationship destroys love, destroys the very possibility of its birth. One thing.

Second thing. You say :

HOW TO KNOW WHEN IT IS APPROPRIATE TO END A LOVE RELATIONSHIP?

As far as I know, Mantra is still alone. As far as I know, it will be very difficult for her to move in love — that's what my feeling is about her. Whenever I have looked into her eyes, I have found a very stony heart. In fact, the relationship has not even started and she is asking how to end it. Clever mind. Wants to have everything clear. Even before it has started, you want to be certain how to end it.

Fear of going into love is such that one wants to be perfectly alert and capable so that if things are too much and one needs to get out, one knows when and how to know when it is time to get out. And Mantra has not yet entered into love and she is asking how to end it! She wants to know every possibility beforehand. She wants to go into it prepared — and nobody can go prepared into a love relationship.

Nobody can go prepared. When you are too much prepared, that very preparedness prevents. Love has to happen! When it happens it is almost from the unknown. It comes... surrounds you... drives you crazy... into unknown directions... into unknown dimensions. It takes you away. It is ALWAYS a surprise. You cannot plan for it. The more you plan for it, the less is the possibility of its happening.

And that's what Mantra is doing — planning, thinking about it, brooding, preparing. And now this is the last thing that one can ask : HOW TO KNOW WHEN IT IS APPROPRIATE TO END A LOVE RELATIONSHIP? It has not even started! The marriage has not happened and you have gone to the lawyer to ask about divorce.

And third thing : love happens on its own and ends on its own. You need not be worried about it. You CANNOT MAKE it happen and you cannot end it. It is beyond you. It is far bigger than you. Your ego is not capable of controlling it. And this is why Mantra is not moving into love energy, and is completely unaware of what it is. She keeps herself in control. She IS a disciplined lady. If she had been around in the old days she would have been appreciated very much — she is a lady. Now she has fallen in wrong company here. This place is not for ladies and gentlemen. For ladies and gentlemen there are other places — cemeteries. This place is for people who are alive — for men, for women, certainly, but not for ladies and gentlemen.

A lady is such a diluted woman — it is worthless. A gentleman is no more a man at all — that's why he is called 'gentleman'. He has lost all energy; he is lukewarm, he has no fire any more, no passion. His fire has gone out. He is mannerly, he knows all about etiquette, but he is dead.

One cannot start love. It is not like a switch that you put on and off. You can only make yourself available : when it happens, it happens. It always comes from the blue — and like a jolt it comes. And it shakes you and uproots you — it is an earthquake. The ground beneath your feet disappears. Suddenly you are falling into a bottomless abyss.

That's why love has been called 'falling in love'. You lose balance. You are no more yourself. You are drunk. You walk like a drunkard. The control, the discipline, can't exist with love. You cannot begin it — how can you end it?

Sometimes it happens : love has ended and you can go on living with the man or the woman, but love has ended. Sometimes the opposite also happens : the woman has died, but love continues; the man has died, but love continues. The ways of love are very mysterious.

You can go on living with the woman and the man, and you can go on reproducing children, and love is not there. Or, the woman has left you, has gone with somebody else; for her, love has taken a different route — but you go on crying for her, you go on feeling for her; your heart still spins and weaves for her. Your heart still sings and dances for her.

Or the woman is dead and there is no possibility of meeting her again, but still it continues.

Love's ways are beyond you. It is not possible for you to know when it is appropriate. Love is such a dangerous thing — you cannot know the appropriate time to begin it, and you cannot find the appropriate time to stop it. It happens in inappropriate times — when you were not even waiting, not thinking, and even when you feel embarrassed. But the God of love takes possession of you.

If you want to start it and end it according to you, then it will not be love. It will be something plastic, synthetic.

HOW TO KNOW WHEN IT IS APPROPRIATE TO END A LOVE RELATIONSHIP? HOW CAN ONE GO DEEP WITH A PERSON WHEN HE IS AFRAID?

That's HIS problem that he is afraid. You need not be worried about it. Never ask about problems which are not yours.

Now, if you choose a person who is afraid, that simply means YOU have some problem deep down, that's why you choose a person who is afraid. Maybe you are afraid and you don't want to go with a courageous person, because then he will take you into unknown territories. So you manage a relationship.

Remember: only relationships can be managed. You manage a relationship with a coward. You know that he will not go very far; you know that "He is more of a coward than me." You know that he will become a hen-pecked husband, that "He will follow me like a shadow." Now this is a problem, a dilemma.

Nobody, not even the wife, loves the hen-pecked husband, cannot — because love always longs for something great. Love always longs for the divine. Now the hen-pecked husband looks so ugly, so unloving, unworthy of love. Even the wife cannot love him.

A woman who is just a slave to you, how can you love her? Love happens amongst friends, not between masters and slaves. You cannot love a woman who is a slave. You can order her, but you cannot love her; you can USE her but you cannot love her. It will be a kind of prostitution, it cannot be love. One loves only equals.

So, Mantra, I don't know about whom you are asking, but that is his problem. He should come to me; he can inquire. But one thing is certain about you: if you fall with a man who is afraid of going into depth, then really you are afraid of going into depth — that's why you have chosen the man.

We always choose the person according to our innermost characteristics. We always fall in love with a person because our mind only allows that.

I have heard about a man who divorced eight times, and again and again was surprised that he always found the same type of woman. And eight times he tried — he tried hard! What more can you do? After each one or two years, he divorced the woman, started looking, and was very alert that he should never fall in the same trap, but again, after six months, eight months, he would find a woman.... For a few days things would go okay... and then the same rut, and he would see that he had again found the same type of woman.

After eight marriages he became aware of the fact that "The real problem is with MY type. Only THESE women appeal to me, and unless I change my type, just changing the woman is not going to help."

You have a certain type of mind; for that mind a certain type of man or woman looks appealing. And you will find him or her again and again — unless you change.

You ask : HOW CAN ONE GO DEEP WITH A PERSON WHEN HE IS AFRAID?

Why did you choose this man? You can choose the dangerous kind — if you want to go really deep.

And EVERYBODY is afraid of going deep — because in depth is death, because every depth relaxes you so much that it looks like death. Every depth takes you out of the ego. That's why people are afraid of love. They hanker for relationship, but they are afraid of love.

And a love which is open-ended creates more fear — because one never knows where it is going to land you. To remain open-ended, to remain in love without creating a relationship, takes real courage. And if you have that courage, love will come in a thousand and one ways, will sing a thousand and one songs in your heart, will dance in a thousand and one ways in your being.

The last question :

Why can't I follow someone who knows? What is the
need to search for truth myself?

HOW ARE YOU GOING TO KNOW THAT THE OTHER KNOWS? It will be just a belief. How are you going to know that the other has known the truth? You don't have any experience. The other may be deceiving — or may himself be deceived. The other may be mad or may be cunning. How are you going to decide that the other has REALLY known? There is no way.

Out of fear you can follow the other, but you will be following blindly. And who knows? The one you are following may be blind himself; he may be following somebody else. That's how things are. That's how priests go on following each other. Nobody knows when the man with the eyes was there.

For example, Jesus was the man with eyes, but then the Christian priests during these two thousand years have been following each other... a long line of blind people. The blind leading the blind.

You ask : WHY CAN'T I FOLLOW SOMEONE WHO KNOWS?

And EVEN if someone knows — for the argument's sake, let us accept that someone knows — even then he cannot transfer his truth to you. He can only indicate the way; you will have to go on the way. He can only give you a prescription; you will have to follow the prescription, you will have to DO things.

Truth cannot be transferred — you will have to arrive at it on your own.

WHAT IS THE NEED TO SEARCH FOR TRUTH MYSELF?

Because without truth life is meaningless. Because truth is always individual; it is not a collective phenomenon. Truth does not belong to the crowd. Each one has to come to it on his own.

Remember, borrowed knowledge is not going to help. It may even be that the man you borrowed your knowledge from was a real knower, but the moment the knowledge comes to you it is borrowed — and borrowed knowledge is always false. The source may have been true but the moment it comes into you, you are untrue, it becomes untrue.

For the truth to exist in you, you will have to become true yourself. One has to go into one's own being to find the truth.

And without truth there is no joy. And without truth there is no significance. And without truth you live in vain.

Two tramps were talking. One, who was skinny and starved, said, "Hey, how come you always look so well-fed and never seem to go hungry?"

The second said, "I've got me this system. I get some horse manure off the road, go up to one of the great big fine houses, knock on the door, and ask for a bit of salt and pepper to put on it. Of course, the people always say, 'You can't eat that! Come on inside for a decent meal.' Or they give me a few rupees and I go eat at a cafe."

So the skinny tramp thought he'd give it a try. He found some really, really old manure, knocked on the door of the biggest house on the street, and said, "Excuse me, lady, could you spare me a pinch of salt and pepper for my bit of food here?"

"You can't eat that, you poor man!" said the woman.

"It's working," thought the tramp, pleased with himself.

"No, you can't eat that," repeated the woman, "you'll be ill! Go round to the stables and get yourself a fresh bit!"

CHAPTER 9

This Very Ancientmost
New Commune

The first question :

Why can't I know God?

 OR YOU ARE IT! Knowledge is not possible. Knowledge pre-supposes division, split. The knower has to be separate from the known. That's why God cannot be known.

You can be God — you are — but you cannot know Him. The very effort to know Him is based on separation. Knowledge separates, divides; it never bridges you. That's why I insist again and again : Be innocent, not knowledgeable — then you will be in harmony with existence. Then you will be existence! Be ignorant. Blessed are the ignorant.

Why? Because when there is no knowledge, no effort to know, divisions disappear. You merge... you meet... you become one.

You cannot know God because God is hiding in you. God cannot be reduced to an object. God cannot become the known. God is the KNOWER; God is your subjectivity. It is not the goal, it is the seeker. It is not at the end of the journey, it is in the beginning — in the very beginning. It is the beginning of the journey... it is the pilgrimage.

So don't try to know God, otherwise you will fail and there will be great frustration.

Become God! Be God! And when I say become God, I am using language which is not adequate. YOU ARE GOD! Recognize it — that's all that I mean by becoming it. LOOK within yourself. Don't seek God — FIND Him! Without seeking He has to be found. All search leads astray, because the search starts from the very false idea that He is separate, that He is far away, that He is somebody else.

He is in the seeker — He is the search!

The second question :

Please explain 'right-mindfulness'. If not a goal or something to practise, what is it?

SAMBUDDHA, 'RIGHT-MINDFULNESS' IS A STRANGE WORD. First : there is no mind in it — hence it is called 'right-mindfulness'. Secondly, there is nothing right and wrong in it — hence it is called right-mindfulness. This is a Buddhist way of saying things.

It can't be a goal, because when there is a goal you are always in the wrong. Why are you in the wrong when there is a goal? because when there is a goal there is desire, when there is desire you are unhappy, discontented. When there is desire, there is anxiety — whether you will be able to make it or not? Will it be possible or not?

When there is desire there is future, and with the future anxiety enters into your being. With the desire you have lost contact with the present.

Right-mindfulness is not a goal, cannot be a goal —because when ALL desires disappear and all goals disappear and you are herenow... that is the moment of right-mindfulness.

Why is it called 'right'? It is called right because it knows no division between right and wrong. Nothing is wrong! and nothing is right. All judgements have disappeared. One is utterly innocent.

When you see a roseflower, does the idea arise in you : "It is right, it is wrong"? When you see the morning star disappearing, does the idea arise in you : "Is it right or is it wrong?" When you start looking at life with no judgement, with no prejudice, then you are in the state of right-mindfulness.

Jesus has said : Judge ye not. Jesus has also said : Resist not evil — not even evil has to be resisted, then arises right-mindfulness. When you are neither moral nor immoral, when you are amoral like trees and animals and birds and beasts, when you are like a small innocent child who has just opened his eyes, with no ideas... then, in that silence, in that purity, it is right-mindfulness.

Why is it called right? It is called right because now it knows nothing as right and wrong — it knows no division, it is indivisible. The acceptance is total! — that's why it is called right. You have fallen into the suchness of existence. You are no longer standing there like a judge.

Judging is wrong. To be in a state of NON-judgement is right. Right, NOT against wrong — right because all wrong and right have disappeared. You have no opinion. You don't carry a philosophy in the mind. You are simply a mirror!

When you come before the mirror, the mirror does not say, "You are beautiful, you are ugly" — it simply reflects. It reflects without condemnation, without appreciation — it reflects choicelessly. It JUST reflects.

When your consciousness has become a mirror and simply reflects whatsoever is the case, it is right-mindfulness. That mirrorlike quality....

And it is not a goal, because EVERY goal will bring dust on the mirror. Every goal will stir desires, and desires surround your mirror like mist — then reflection is not true, then suchness is not reflected. When you have some idea, you cannot be true to reality. You distort reality according to your idea. You try to mould reality according to your idea. You are to modify reality. You go on looking for your idea. You are searching for support : you would like reality to support YOUR idea, you would like reality to agree with you — and then you distort. Then you start seeing things which are not there, and you stop seeing things which ARE there. Then you start living in a mind-world.

To live in the mind is wrong. To live without mind is right, because without mind, the consciousness exists in its purity, mirror-like — it simply reflects. It says nothing! It has NO interpretation. It interprets not.

And why is it called mindfulness? This is the translation of a Buddhist term SAMMASATI. SAMMA means right — the translation is not very correct, cannot be. SAMMA is a very strange word, very significant, has many meanings; 'right' is only one of its meanings. SAMMA is the root from where SAMADHI arises; the word SAMADHI comes from SAMMA.

SAMMA means many things. One : tranquillity, silence, equanimity, balance, undisturbedness, undistractedness, centredness, groundedness — they are all aspects of SAMMA. 'Right' is a very poor translation of SAMMA.

And SATI — SAMMASATI. SATI can mean mindfulness, can mean remembrance, can mean reflection, can mean recollectedness, can mean presence. All those meanings are involved in it. Mindfulness is only one of the meanings. It is a very potential and pregnant word — SAMMASATI.

It is the seventh step in Buddha's eight steps — you are very close to reality. The eighth is samadhi. The seventh is SAMMASATI. You have come very very close; you are just on the threshold of reality — it has to be very very significant. When you are utterly present in the presence, when you don't have any past and don't have any future... when this cuckoo calling, this train passing, this dog barking, is all... when THIS is all and there is no that, when the word 'here' is your whole reality and there is no there, when now contains ALL time and there is no then... then you are in the state of SAMMASATI.

That's what I go on calling 'herenow' — that is SAMMASATI. Then you are utterly present, absolutely present. When something is going on in your mind about the past, you are not here; a part of you is travelling towards the past, and a part of you is travelling towards the future — only a small fragment is here.

When ALL the parts of your being are here, when you are totally at home, nothing is missing, when you are integratedly here, then it is right-mindfulness. In that moment you will reflect reality — as it is, without any distraction, without any distortion. Because you don't have any thought in the mind, how can you distort it? Thought distorts, thinking is destructive. It goes on imposing — it does not allow you to see that which is.

Right-mindfulness is a state of no-mind, no-thought!

And remember : it is also a state of no-feeling — otherwise, you may think it is a state of feeling. No, it is not — because feeling again creates ripples and the surface of the lake is disturbed, and again the moon is not reflected as it is.

Neither thought disturbs you, nor feeling.

These are the three states : one is thinking — the most disturbed state; second is feeling — less disturbed than thinking, but still disturbed; third is being — no disturbance at all. One is in the head, second is in the heart, third is in your guts. Right-mindfulness is a gut-state : no head, no heart. You are simply there undefined, undefinable.

Sambuddha, you ask me :

PLEASE EXPLAIN WHAT 'RIGHT-MINDFULNESS' IS. IF NOT A GOAL OR SOMETHING TO PRACTISE, WHAT IS IT?

And, yes, it is not a practice. You cannot practise it, because practice brings goal! Practice is desire, practice is mind. And remember : whenever you practise something, you are imposing something against yourself, otherwise why practise it? against whom are you practising? When you practise truth, what will you do? You will repress the untruth — but the untruth will remain there, deep inside you, ready to explode any moment. It will go on accumulating.

When you practise love, what will you do? You will repress hatred. When you practise compassion, what will you do? You will repress anger. And all that is repressed will go on remaining in you, and all that is practised will remain on the surface, and all that is rejected will go deep into your being. The rejected will become part of your being and the practised will remain just a coating, a painting on the surface.

And remember : whenever you practise anything, you are angry at it. Naturally so — because all practising divides you, makes you schizophrenic. One part of you is trying to manipulate the other part. One part of you is trying to enforce some ideas on the other part. And the part that is trying to enforce is a very impotent part, but articulate — your head. It has NO power, but it is very articulate, very clever, very cunning, very argumentative.

And the head goes on imposing on your body, on your heart, which are far more potential, far more powerful; they have energy sources, but they are not articulate, they are not argumentative — they are silent. And the head goes on pretending that it has practised... and then a situation arises and all practice is thrown away — because the head has no energy.

You think for years that you will never be angry, then one day somebody insults you and in a single moment you have forgotten all that practice. And you ARE angry! By the time you come to know that you are angry, anger has already happened. You are burning, you are fire. From where does this fire come? And YEARS of practice! That practice was just on the surface. Mind was pretending; because there was no situation provoking you, mind was able to pretend. Now the situation has arisen and mind is not able to pretend. The reality asserts itself.

That's why down the ages, through the ages, the so-called religious people have been escaping from society, from life. Why? They are escaping from situations where their practice can be proved wrong; nothing else are they doing. Going to the Himalayas they are simply escaping from the world — because the world brings situations! And their so-called practice and their religion and their discipline is broken again and again. Somebody insults, or a beautiful woman passes by, and all their celibacy and all their brahmacharya and all their ideas are gone. A single beautiful woman is enough to destroy all their years of celibacy.

They escape from women, they escape from the world, they escape from money and the market — they know that they can be moral and religious and saintly only when there is no situation which provokes their reality. Then the mind can go on playing the game in a monastery. When there is no challenge, mind seems to be the master. When there is challenge, mind is no more a master.

Whatsoever you practise remains false. Never out of practice has anything real happened. Beware of this. The real happens only through understanding, not through practice. And what is the difference?

Understanding will say : Remain where situations arise, remain where challenges surround you. Be there where provocations and temptations exist. Test yourself there. Go into situations! Understanding will say : If anger comes, then GO into anger and see what it is. See yourself — don't trust anybody else's judgement about it. Go into it! Be burnt by it. Let it leave scars on your being — because one learns only through the hard way. Only your experience will tell you again and again and again that anger is stupid — not that it is a sin! it is simply stupid. And as the understanding grows deeper, anger will be coming less and less. One day... the understanding has touched your very core of being, the light has penetrated you. You have seen through and through that anger is futile : in that very moment anger has disappeared and there has not been any repression.

Remember this : repression is the pitfall for ALL those people who want to transform their lives — they have to avoid repression. Indulgence is not so bad, because indulgence can one day bring understanding, but repression can never bring understanding. How can you understand something which you go on repressing and you don't look into? — you go on covering it, go on throwing it in the basement of your being.

And remember : the more you practise, the more you pretend, the more you are angry at your own practice. Your real parts, your guts are angry.

The intellectual young man was telling off his girlfriend. "Jane," he remonstrated, "I don't think you are the girl for me. My interests are in art, literature and in music. You are only concerned with sports, with gambling and with common activities that are altogether alien to me. In fact, to be blunt about it — you are downright uncouth!"

"Uncouth!" she exploded. "Me?! WHAT ARE YOU TALKING ABOUT? Uncouth? Didn't I go along with you to them operas, them concerts, them lectures, and all that sort of shit?!"

That's what will happen. You can go on practising, but deep down you know that you are repressing, that you are rejecting, that you are denying some essential parts of your being.

Right-mindfulness is the flavour of understanding, not the outcome of practice. Right-mindfulness is the fragrance — the fragrance of seeing into things deeply, the fragrance of insight.

The third question:

Is there any pain worse than this? You have touched my secret: All my sources are poisoned and yet I manage to go on living and it is not possible — that is what I want to hide from everyone. You put the finger on my deepest wounds, and make me scream out in pain and then you lead me to the only life-giving source — acceptance. No words any more.
Only tears....

NEERJO, ECSTASY IS ONLY OUT OF AGONY — and the deeper the agony, the deeper the ecstasy will be; total the agony, total will be the ecstasy. Everything has to be paid for. For ecstasy, we have to pay in agony. One has to go through deep pain to get rid of pain. Pain is cleansing. Pain is a fire; it burns the rubbish in you, it destroys the unessential. Just as we purify gold through fire, consciousness is purified through pain. Pain has something to deliver to you.

Don't avoid pain! If you avoid pain, you are avoiding pleasure. Don't avoid the world! If you avoid the world, you have avoided God. Don't avoid darkness. If you avoid darkness, dawn will never come. It is out of the dark night that the morning is born. And when the night is darkest, the sunrise is closest.

Remember this fundamental law of life, this paradox.

If I have to cleanse you, purify you, I have to become a fire to you. Jesus has said: I am fire and I have come to burn you! Every Master is a fire. If you come across a Master who is not a fire, but just a kind of ointment, escape from there! He will give you consolations, but he will not be able to transmute your life-energies. He may be able to make you comfortable in life, but he will not be able to help you to transcend life.

The real Master is always a fire. A real Master is always there to destroy.

Yes, I will touch your wounds again and again, Neerjo. You are hiding them. You are hiding them, that's why they are not healing. They have to be brought to sunlight, to fresh air. They have to be exposed. Only in that exposure will they start healing. And, yes, when I touch your wound it hurts. The more you want to be healed, the more it will hurt, because much pus is there. You have been hiding the wounds for so long — much pus has gathered there. The pus has to be thrown out of your system, the poison has to be thrown out of your system.

This agony is not a curse, it is a blessing — because out of this agony, slowly slowly you will arise in a totally different dimension. Acceptance is the bridge. Accept the pain, accept the wounds, accept yourself as you are! Don't try to pretend to be somebody else, don't try to show that you are not this. Don't be egoistic, and don't go on pretending and laughing while your heart is crying. Don't smile if your eyes are full of tears. Don't be inauthentic, because by being inauthentic you are simply protecting your wounds from being healed. Your whole being will become rotten.

That's how people are! Pus and pus and pus.... And they are somehow managing so that nobody should know how much it stinks inside them. They don't go inside themselves because it stinks too much, it is horrible. And they don't allow anybody to enter their being — that's why they don't love, because love will need exposure. They don't make contact, because if you contact somebody he may smell things that you are hiding. You know. You keep aloof, you go only so far.

You don't go inside yourself, you don't allow anybody else to go inside you. But, Neerjo, when you have come to me you have to allow me to come inside you. That's what sannyas is all about. A declaration that for me your doors are open. By becoming a sannyasin, you have handed the key to me. Now, pain is going to be there, because sannyas is a surgery. Many rotten parts have to be cut and much poison has to be taken out of your system — it is going to be painful. But be courageous. Go through it and great will be your joy.

The fourth question :

Why should one search for god?
Is not life enough?

LIFE IS GOD! GOD IS LIFE! those two words are synonymous, synonyms. Forget about God! Search for life — it is the same search.

Using the word 'God' does not change anything. But I know why the question has arisen. The question has arisen because the priests have been telling you that life and God are not only separate but opposite. They have been telling you that if you want to search and seek God, you will have to renounce life — hence the question. They have been telling you that God is very angry at you because you are living, God is very angry at you because you are loving, God is very angry at you that you are happy here on this earth. Be sad! be miserable! and pray and ask for the other world. Feel yourself a stranger here; feel as if you have been thrown into a prison. This is a kind of punishment, this life.

That's what your priests have been telling you down the ages. They have created the idea, a very false idea and a very irreligious idea, that God and life are not only separate but antagonistic. If you search for life, you will be against God. If you want to search for God, you have to be against life. Now this is utter stupidity! God is life, God is the very centre of life. Life is the circumference of God's centre. Life is the cyclone and God is the centre of the cyclone.

Searching for God you will come to know the deepest meaning of life. Searching for life you will start falling into God unawares. If you go deep into life, you will find God. If you go deep into God, you will find life abundant.

But the religious people have destroyed a beautiful word — 'God' is a beautiful word, but it has been used by wrong people. It has become associated with wrong meanings. When I use the word 'God', I mean the innermost core of life — not that you have to renounce life, but that you have to love life, that you have to dive deep into life.

Why do I use the word 'God'? Why can't I drop it and simply use 'life'? The problem is that with life you have the idea that life finishes in the mundane — the market, the money, the power, the prestige, the politics, the family, and the rut and the routine. You think this is life. This is just the very periphery of life. You are standing in the porch and you think this is the palace. It is part of the palace, but it is just the entrance. There are great treasures in the palace.

That's why I don't use just the word 'life', because that will give you again a wrong notion. So I have to go on using both the words : life and God — and go on insisting that they are synonyms.

Search for the centre of life and you will be searching for God.

Jesus has said : Seek ye first the Kingdom of God, then all else shall be added unto you. Life comes on its own — all else shall be added unto you. If you seek the centre, then the periphery follows, the circumference follows. When you are standing at the centre, the whole life is available to you. But it is not so if you are standing on the circumference. You may not be even aware of the centre.

From the centre, the circumference remains available; but from the circumference you may not even become alert, you may not be even conscious that there is a centre also.

I have heard a beautiful story :

Once Haroun-Al Rashid, the Caliph of Baghdad, was celebrating a royal occasion. He ordered a grand display of all manner of jewellery and artwork for the occasion, and invited not only courtiers and nobles but many commoners also.

At the height of the celebrations, the Sultan developed a magnanimous mood and all of a sudden he ordered every person present to touch any article they liked, and that article, no matter how precious, would belong to that person. No sooner was the royal command given than a rush was made to possess the costliest thing within reach.

A beautiful slave girl, remaining composed and serene by the side of the throne asked the Sultan to reaffirm his command. On receiving affirmation, the slave girl immediately touched the Caliph himself on the arm saying, "Why should I run after those things when the master of them all is here?"

The Sultan, in admiration of the insight shown by the girl, complimented her and said, "Now that you possess me, the whole of my kingdom is yours."

Life is the circumference : God is the centre. If you touch God, all is yours; if you have arrived at the centre, then the whole belongs to you.

You ask : WHY SHOULD ONE SEARCH FOR GOD? IS NOT LIFE ENOUGH?

You will know life only when you have touched God. By being divine, life will be revealed to you in all its dimensions. It has multi-facets to it, it is multi-dimensional. Just eating, drinking and merrying is not all. And I am not against it, remember! It is perfectly good as it is. It is beautiful as it is, but it is not all.

I am a spiritual hedonist. I am a synthesis of Buddha and Epicurus. Nobody has tried that yet. There have been people who are absolutely concerned with eating, drinking and merrying, and they don't bother a bit about God and all that nonsense. There are people who are absolutely concerned with God and don't bother about eating, drinking and merrying and all that nonsense. I love both. I am totally in love with both. And I don't see any contradiction between the two.

Eating, drinking, merrying, is the circumference. It is good! God IS there too, but very dilute. When you start moving towards the centre, God becomes more concentrated. When you drink, you attain to a forgetfulness which is momentary. When you drink out of God, you attain to a forgetfulness which is eternal. When you fall in love with somebody's body, it is going to be a very temporary affair. When you fall in love with somebody's spirit, it is going to be an eternal phenomenon. Loving the body is good, but nothing compared with the love of the soul. Loving the visible is good, but don't get caught there — there is more to it. Hiding behind it is the invisible.

Eating is joyful, but when you start eating consciousness... that is what meditation is. When you start nourishing consciousness, then you know what real eating is. That's what Jesus said to his disciples when he was departing : Eat me, drink me — let me be your food. Each disciple has to become a cannibal because he has to eat the Master. And each Master is already a skilled cannibal — he goes on eating his disciples.

There are things on the periphery, and there are things at the centre. The circumference cannot exist without the centre and the centre cannot exist without the circumference. That's why I say they both are together, they are part of each other.

Epicurus lives on the circumference. Buddha lives at the centre. I live together in both the spaces. And that is my message to you : Be available to the circumference as much as to the centre; and go on moving in and out. Fall in love and meditate! Be in the body and be the soul! Be the visible and be the invisible! And you will be the richest sannyasins that have ever existed on this earth.

Epicurus' followers were rich — they knew how to eat and drink and be merry; but they were a little poor in the sense that they didn't know how to meditate. They knew how to love, how to relate, but they were not aware at all that there exists something like meditation. And they were beautiful people! Their dance was something of the eternal, but they were not aware of the eternal. Their joy was a reflection of something very deep, but they were not aware of the depth. They lived on the waves — although the waves were living on the ocean, in the ocean, but they lived on the waves. They sailed in small boats, and they were happy with the sun and the sea, and their joy was great, and I am ALL for it — but there are deeper treasures also. There are pearls which can only be found by diving.

Buddha's followers dived deep into the sea and forgot all about the sun and the waves and the joy and surfing — they forgot all about that. They were rich; they attained to the centre — but they were poor also.

My own approach is that there is no need to choose — be choicelessly available to all. Sometimes it is good to be on the waves, in the sun, and sometimes it is good to go to the depth, to the pacific depth of life, to those dark silences where the sun has never penetrated. To be available to both the world and God, life and God, is freedom. To me, the Epicureans are not free because they cannot go into the depth; and Buddhists are not free either because they cannot go back to the surface. Their freedom has limitations.

I give you absolute freedom without any limitations; I make available to you all that God has made available to you. You are the most courageous experiment on the earth hitherto! It needs guts to be available to these two places together — it needs guts to be in love and still be in meditation, to meditate and yet to love. It is very easy, comfortable, to be in love and forget about meditation; it is simple, it has no complexity in it — because when you love, you forget yourself, you remember the other, you become other-oriented. It is a simple process to forget yourself and to become other-oriented. To love and to meditate is difficult, complex, because to meditate means to forget the other and become self-oriented. Now you will be moving between polarities — you will have to become a swinger. But out of complexity is richness.

Osho, Whenever I am with somebody funny,
I become funny.
With somebody sad, I feel sad,
Somebody ecstatic, I feel blissful,
And with a real schmuck,
I become a schmuck too.
And sitting with you in lecture,
enlightenment.
What is happening?
And where is me?

CHAITANYA HARI, I MUST MAKE YOU AWARE that you are very close to enlightenment. If you want to escape, escape now — otherwise it will be too late!

It is beautiful... the ego is disappearing. That's how it should be! You are melting; you are no more an iceberg. You are becoming a mirror! — so somebody is sad, you reflect sadness; and somebody is ecstatic and you express ecstasy. And somebody is dancing and a dance arises in you. And somebody sings a song and you echo it. You are becoming a mirror!

Don't be afraid, don't be worried, don't create a problem out of it. Relax into it... this is how it should be.

Forget about yourself. Don't ask : AND WHERE IS ME? 'Me' is a false entity, it is a shadow, it is illusion... it IS disappearing. You are becoming a hollow bamboo. It will be frightening, because to you it will look as if you are dying. In fact, it is true that you are dying — the ego is dying. It is true that you will not be able to feel your personality. How can you feel your personality? — when somebody laughs, there is laughter in you, and somebody cries and tears come to you. How can you feel your personality?

A personality means resistance : somebody is crying and you are still happy — that is personality. Somebody is laughing and you are still crying that is personality. You are separate, that is personality — you resist. You demark yourself. You say, "I am THIS, and I will remain this. You can go on laughing — I don't care. I am sad and I won't allow you to disturb my sadness. I will persist. This is ME!"

The ego is like ice, frozen. It is a resistance, a continuous resistance.

Now that is dissolving — you are blessed, Chaitanya Hari. Help it to go. Soon greater things will happen. Looking at a tree you will become a tree; you will forget to go back to your room and Krishna will have to come and find you.

It happened to Socrates : one night he went outside and he started looking at the stars and he became a star. He was looking at a star and it was fascinating. It was so beautiful that he could not look away from it. He became one with it. And the snow started falling and he was frozen — he was almost dead by the morning when he was found. His disciples searched for him the whole night; only in the morning was he found, covered with snow... but still his eyes were looking at the sky. He was not there! They had to shake him and shock him and warm him and massage him to come back. Slowly, slowly, he came back and they asked, "What has happened?"

And he laughed. He said, "This is strange! I became the star."

That used to happen to Ramakrishna almost every day. Anywhere, any excuse, and he would fall into samadhi. For hours. Walking on the road, his disciples were always in trouble. Even somebody passing by, and in India just anybody can say, HARE KRISHNA, HARE RAMA... just any word that reminded him of God. People ordinarily salute in India : JAI RAMJI — hail God! Anybody. And Ramakrishna coming — anybody would say it. Just hearing the word 'Ram' and he is gone! standing on the road, in the middle of the traffic. And the crowd gathers, and the policeman comes and tells the disciples : "Take your Master away from here!" And they have to carry his body and he is just gone. Enough it was!

Once it happened that for six days continuously he remained

like a corpse. His disciples had to feed him, to wash him, and cry and pray to God, "Send our Master back!"

Yes, it is possible. Standing by the side of a pine tree, you can become a pine. Touching a rock, you can become a rock — because really there are no divisions. We are part of one reality. WE ARE NOT APART! — we are one with the whole.

When somebody is crying, you are crying. And when somebody is dancing, you are dancing. We are joined together. We are interlinked. We are not independent, we are not dependent either — we are interdependent. One consciousness, one life, surrounds you, within and without. It is oneness.

Something beautiful is very close by — if you can allow it, you will be gone and God will be there. But it almost always happens that in such moments one becomes very frightened. One starts asking: "And where is me?" When resistance starts disappearing and personality starts disappearing, naturally one becomes frightened: "What is happening to me? Am I going mad? Why should I cry if somebody else is crying?" — because you have been taught that you are separate. But that teaching is simply false; it is a make-believe.

And for one reason more there will be fear: because now there are so many people — somebody is crying and somebody is laughing, now what will you do? You will have to cry and laugh together. And then people will certainly think you have gone mad! It is okay that somebody is crying and you feel empathy and you cry, and somebody is laughing, naturally laughter is infectious and you start laughing. But what will you do when one person is crying and another person is laughing? And if you do both together you are very contradictory — but that's what is possible. That is divine madness; that is the greatest experience that is possible to man. Allow that too!

That is my purpose here. Why am I creating this commune? Just to create a certain milieu where everything is allowed, nobody interferes. If you are crying and laughing together, nobody comes and condemns you; people respect you, they have reverence for you. They know that something is happening to you; they will not interpret and they will not condemn — not even in their eyes will there be any indication that this is not good.

That is a spiritual community: where all is allowed, unconditionally; where everybody is helped into whatsoever space he is moving; where all kinds of spaces are respected; where nobody enforces any particular pattern and particular character. And all kinds of things are going to happen in my commune, because I am making available to you ALL the paths that have happened in the past, AND things which are going to happen in the future too.

So, many things are going to happen. Somebody may become a Socrates and somebody may become a Ramakrishna and somebody may become a Mahavir and somebody may become a Buddha and somebody a Meera and somebody a Jesus — all that is possible. You ALL are carrying seeds for that. Just right soil is needed and you will start sprouting. You need support.

So support! If something is happening to somebody, even if your old mind brings interpretations, drop that mind; be respectful to the person and the space that he is moving in.

Now, if you find Chaitanya Hari somewhere crying and laughing together, help him, tickle him, make him cry, so that he can go as deep as possible. All kinds of experiences have to be gone through, only then one day does one transcend experiences. Then a day arrives when you have passed through experiencing.

Then somebody cries and nothing happens to you, and somebody laughs and nothing happens to you... then simply nothing happens to you because you have become a nothing. But before that this is going to happen, that you will be affected, that you will become very vulnerable, that you will start soaking everything that is around you, that you will start becoming all kinds of things. That you will be very much confused! That there will be CHAOS in you — but remember, only out of chaos are stars born. And one has to be ready to go into chaos.

When you come back, all will be gone. Then nothingness

pervades. Buddha has called that nothingness 'nirvana'. Then nothing affects, because there is nobody to be affected and there is nobody to affect. Then all is a dream and you are just a witness to it....

The sixth question :

Osho, as more people come and take sannyas and more days pass, it seems that many of us grow together — stronger and stronger without even meeting much.

It seemed to me when you spoke of the 'new community' that somehow it is an old community of friends, reuniting again through your love and grace.

Thank you, Osho.

YES, PRASAD, that's how it is. Many of you have been with me in the past. Many of you have been together with each other in the past. It is a meeting of old friends. You have forgotten — I have not forgotten. And sooner or later you will also start remembering.

This new commune is going to be one of the oldest things on the earth, very ancientmost. And travellers from different paths have come — travellers from different directions and dimensions. Jews are here and Mohammedans are here and Hindus and Jains and Buddhists and Christians and Taoists — all kinds of people are here. All cultures are meeting here; all religions pouring into each other.

And a natural synthesis will arise. We are not creating any synthesis, but it is happening on its own.

The universal man can be born only out of such a commune — the man who will not be a Christian and will not be a Jew and will not be a Hindu and will not be Indian and will not be Chinese and will not be German. All boundaries are dissolving here.

And you are certainly not new. You have been here long enough, you have lived long enough. Many many lives you have been passing. And you have brought many riches; you have brought great heritages with you. And once all those heritages are poured into one pool, it will be one of the richest phenomena that has ever happened or can ever happen.

The seventh question :

Sometimes I feel so jealous of all those people who live close to you — the ones in Lao Tzu House and those who see you every night in darshan. I tell myself that Lao Tzu House is in my own heart, but this is just knowledge. Just going through the gates of your house is like falling into another world — I can feel it. And to live there with you must be like a miracle. Meanwhile, I eat my heart out.

PREM GARJAN, YOU ARE FORTUNATE that you are not in the Lao Tzu house — for many reasons. One is : those who are in the Lao Tzu house, I torture them very much — you don't know about it outside. They are continuously crucified. Sooner or later, I am going to make my whole campus Lao Tzu house so everybody will be inside — and then you will know.

Meanwhile, enjoy as much as you can.

And secondly, what almost always happens is : when you are too close to me you start forgetting about me. That too is a misfortune. When you are for twenty-four hours in the same place where I am, naturally you start taking my presence for granted. You become oblivious. That's how the human mind functions.

The gardener who lives the whole day in the garden has stopped seeing the trees long ago. The man who lives in the Himalayas knows nothing of the beauty of the Himalayas. When you go to the Himalayas, you know the beauty of it. But if you start living there, how long will you be able to know the beauty of it? After a few days the honeymoon is over — and then those Himalayan peaks are taken for granted. Not that they have become less beautiful — they are exactly the same — but you have become insensitive.

The obvious is almost always forgotten.

That's how we have forgotten God! because we LIVE IN HIS HOUSE, and He is ALWAYS around — and we have forgotten about Him.

Go and ask the fish in the ocean — the fish has forgotten about the ocean. The fish only knows, Garjan, when it is thrown out of the ocean, when it is on the sands, in the sun — then it knows what the ocean was, what the ocean is. Now it is thirsty for the ocean. Now there is great longing for the ocean. But it has lived in the ocean for years and it has not even thought for a single moment, it has not even thanked God for the whole ocean that was given to her.

That's how it happens. It is very natural to our minds because our minds are not very sensitive, they are very dull.

You love a woman — there is great joy; you feel so happy. And then the woman starts living with you and after a few days you have forgotten about her! You don't even look at her! Still you touch her hand, but nothing flows. She has forgotten you, you have forgotten her. Familiarity makes people very unfamiliar. And the obvious becomes non-existential.

I have heard :

In an anthropological institute in Vienna, there used to be great interest in the various love postures of the races. Two professors, one a Frenchman and the other a German, devoted most of their waking hours to the matter, consulting such ancient texts as *THE KAMASUTRA* and *THE PERFUMED GARDEN*. When they finally conferred to compare notes, they disagreed on only one point : the German said there were 138 postures; the Frenchman claimed there were 139. A hot argument ensued. It was decided to enumerate the positions.

"Well," the Frenchman began, "first, of course, there is the good old way."

"Ach!" exclaimed the German professor disgustedly. "You win — I forgot about that one."

And the last question :

Osho, you are here — then why do I still go on
doubting?

This anecdote :

Sinclair had been married for ten years and had lived all of them in agony. He was unbelievably jealous of his coquettish wife; for years he had suspected she was having an affair with his business partner. Finally, he could stand the tension no longer and hired a detective to trail her.

A few days later, the detective reported to Sinclair.

"Well, did you follow them?"

"Oh, yes," said the detective. "I have the report here. Last night she left your home about eight thirty, and then she met a man on the corner of Reid Street and Montgomery Place. They strolled around for about fifteen minutes, then they got into a car and went down to Patmore Lane. There they parked for a half hour and he made advances to her to which she ungrudgingly responded. Then they drove to the Franconia Hotel; checked at the desk and found out that they were occupying room 301. Fortunately, room 301 faced the street, so I climbed a tree opposite their window, peered in and saw them both standing there completely nude, fondling each other..."

"And then?!" cried Mr. Sinclair. "What happened then?"

"Oh, well, then they pulled down the shade."

"Oh," moaned Sinclair, "what a tragedy! Always to doubt, never to know...!"

I AM HERE, but that will not make much difference — you

have learnt the habit of doubt. It has become ingrained, it has become unconscious. It is not that you doubt — it is that you have become doubt. So even if I am here confronting you, you go on missing me. The doubt goes on arising. If one doubt disappears, you produce another. If that disappears, you produce another. Doubts come to you just like leaves come to a tree.

You will have to see the point. You will have to see me without your doubting mind. What are you expecting? Your expectation is that by and by I will argue against all your doubts, I will prove things so that your doubts are dissolved — then you will be able to see me. That is not going to happen. I can go on and on talking to you, I can go on and on showering myself on you, but that will not help much — the doubting mind will go on creating new doubts, fresh doubts.

If you are waiting for that moment when all doubts are gone, then you will look at me, then that moment will never come — I will be gone. That moment will never come. If you want that moment, then you have to put your doubts aside.

Just once, look at me... without any doubt, and that will suffice. That will trigger a process of trust in you. Only through trust is the meeting with me possible. And only through trust is transformation.

CHAPTER
10

You Can't Win 'em All

The first question :

I'm not skilled in any art. Poetry sometimes happens. Dance happens through me. I feel now there is such a thing as the art of living, of life. Have you a comment?

AMRITA, that is the right way. Poetry cannot be done, it can only be allowed. Poetry is not a technique, you cannot learn it. It is a happening — so is all art. Skill is not the central core of any art. Skill is of course needed, but that is secondary. And if the essential is there, one learns the skill easily, it comes. If the essential is not there, then you can become very skillful, you can know all the technique of it, and still you will never become an artist, you will remain a technician.

And there is NO need to become a technician. Poetry should not be there as a performance — it should be a sheer joy, a celebration of life. You need not bother whether somebody comes to know about your poetry or not.

The wild flower — nobody may come to know about it — still blooms! Be a wild flower. And don't think of exhibitions. Dance as the dance comes to you. There is NO need to be skillful about it. If the skill starts coming to you slowly, slowly, without any effort on your part, that's good; but there is no need to go in search of it.

You say : I AM NOT SKILLED IN ANY ART.

Then art IS possible. The skilled person is a closed person. Have you ever heard of anybody becoming a poet by learning the art of poetry? In fact, the universities and the colleges put people off poetry. The more they teach, the more it becomes impossible for anybody to become a poet. They destroy something rather than create something.

The moment you start thinking about poetry as a craft, as skill, as technique, you have missed the point.

Poetry is like love : you need not learn it. It is LOVE of life! When you are happy, it flows. When you are overflowing, it flows in many ways. Sometimes in colour — painting is poetry in colour. Sometimes in dance — dance is poetry in movement. Sometimes in song... and then by and by it starts transforming your whole life. Then your whole life becomes poetry.

Buddha is poetry lived, so is Jesus.

You say : POETRY SOMETIMES HAPPENS.

Don't hanker and don't desire that it should happen at other times too. If you try for other times too, you will destroy the spontaneity of it. One has to wait. One has to be patient. One has to remain open... just like you wait for a guest : your doors open, you stand on the threshold and you go on looking down the road. Your heart is throbbing. But what else can you do? When the guest comes, the guest comes.

Poetry is a guest — become a host! But don't try to pull, don't try to manipulate — poetry cannot be manufactured. It is not man-made : it is God-made. All poetry has the signature of God; if it is true poetry then it is always God-made.

Yes, you can compose, you can manage to create an appearance of poetry, but it will be false, it will not have life in it, it will not have spirit in it. It will be dead, it will be soul-less.

Wait for those moments... they will be rare, once in a while. But it is good! Poetry is a rare phenomenon; it is not the ordinary rut. The dance will be rare, once in a while, but it HAS to be so! Allow it. When it comes, go totally into it. When it is not coming, don't try to manage it. If you try to manage, you will start creating false things, pseudo things. And not only that : if you manage, those real moments of happening will stop. You will become closed to them.

All desiring is destructive.

And you say : DANCE HAPPENS THROUGH ME.

Right, you are on exactly the right track, Amrita. When dance happens through you, it is divine dance. When YOU dance, it is very ordinary, mundane; it has not the touch of the unknown in it; it has no inspiration. It is just gymnastics, a body exercise — you have learnt a few steps and movements and you are twisting your body. You are not possessed by God!

When a dance comes to you, you are possessed, you are no more yourself. God has penetrated you. Then there is a totally different quality to it. Then you are not the dancer : you are being danced. And the difference is immense. There is no effort on your part. You are simply taken over. You don't know what is happening. You are neither the doer nor the knower, and then something great happens — something which is not of this earth. Those are the religious moments.

A dancer can know God more easily than a thinker. And a painter can know God more easily than a businessman. And a poet is certainly closer to God than any politician. These are the people of God! The artist comes closest.

In a better world, with better understanding, the poet should be the only priest. Only HE can be the priest — not the theologian, nor the trained priest, but a wild poet. That used to be so in primitive societies. It is still so in primitive societies. The madman is the priest, the poet is the priest — the inspired is the priest. He does not preach on his own; he simply lets himself go into the unknown. He becomes possessed. He dances a wild dance, he sings a wild song — for hours — he goes on dancing and dancing. And then there comes a moment when the man disappears and God takes possession. Then his eyes change — they roll upwards. Then his body has a totally different energy. It is felt by the people who are present there — the presence is felt, the transformation is felt. The man is metamorphosed, the man is drunk with the divine, then he speaks — sometimes in a language that cannot be understood, sometimes in words which are not together, with no grammar, with no rules, he utters. But those few words that he utters can become the keys to the unknown, to God.

That's how the Vedas were uttered. That's how the

Upanishads were uttered. That's how Jesus is so beautiful! I have never come across a greater poet than Jesus, although nobody thinks about him as a poet — but he is one of the greatest poets that has ever walked on the earth. Just see the poetry of his sayings — the Sermon on the Mount. Each single word is so full of poetry. He must have been possessed in that moment when he delivered that sermon; God must have spoken through him. He must have been one with God in those moments. It is not HE who is speaking; he is just a vehicle, a passage, a medium, a messenger.

And that is the meaning of the word 'Christ', 'Messiah' — he brings the message. He allows the message to come to you; he becomes a bridge.

So when the poetry comes, let it come. Be thankful. When the dance comes, let it come. Be grateful. But never try to bring it. And I know — the human mind is greedy; it continuously wants more and more. Once something has happened, you want it to be repeated again and again. You will destroy it — don't be greedy!

With greed, God disappears. God is possible only with a non-greedy mind. Hope and wait and pray, but don't be greedy.

And you ask : I FEEL NOW THERE IS SUCH A THING AS THE ART OF LIVING, OF LIFE TOO.

There is no separate art of life. If you know how to allow poetry, if you know how to allow dance, if you know how to allow love — if you know how to ALLOW, then you know the art of life. In the allowing, in the let-go, in the surrender, is the art of life. How not to be and to let God be — that is the only art of life.

And one has to learn through many many ways. Poetry is one way, song is another, dance still another. Learn allowing. Learn receptivity. Learn becoming a womb. Learn to be feminine. Don't be masculine. Don't be aggressive. Don't try to conquer God, life, love, truth! Don't go like a soldier : go like a beloved, a woman.

Science is masculine, religion is feminine. That's why science has destroyed the whole earth — the technology of it has been destructive. The ecology has been disrupted so badly that there seems to be no possibility of putting it right again. The circuit is broken everywhere. And the reason is that science became too much and lost track of the feminine qualities in human consciousness. Man became unbalanced, lopsided.

Religion has to be brought back. And by 'religion' I mean the feminine; by 'religion' I mean receptivity — not going to conquer, but waiting for the guest to come; not doing, but happening.

The second question :

Osho, today after lecture, as I was kneeling before your platform sexual fantasies concerning you filled my head. On the one hand, my body was filled with energy and it felt good, on the other hand I began to feel guilty, that it was wrong to have such thoughts about you and I shouldn't allow them to continue.

Then my stomach began cramping and I had to run to the bathroom with diarrhoea.

What is happening? And is it okay to have such fantasies?

BARKHA, SEX IS AS SACRED AS SAMADHI. The lowest and the highest are part of one continuum. The lowest rung is as much part of the ladder as the highest rung; they are nowhere divided. And if you deny the lower, you will never be able to reach to the higher.

Sex is nothing to feel guilty about! It is your life. It is where you ARE — how can you avoid it? If you avoid it, you will be pseudo, inauthentic, untrue. If you avoid it, if you repress it, you will not be able to move upwards because the energy will be repressed through it.

Right now, it is at the stage of sexuality that you are. When you listen to me, when you start feeling me, naturally your energy is stirred. And it can only be stirred WHERE it is. Listening to me, feeling me, being in love with me, your samadhi cannot bloom right now. But if your sexuality starts moving, that's a good sign. That shows you have been contacted, that something has stirred in you, that something has become a movement in you, that you are no more a stagnant pool, that you have started flowing towards the ocean.

Certainly, the ocean is far away. It will come in the very end. But if you stop this small muddy pool from flowing, you will never reach to the ocean. I know the mud of it, but it has to be accepted. You have to start flowing! Don't be worried about sexual fantasies; they are just natural.

The serpent and the saviour are not two — they are one. In fact, there is an ancient tradition that says that when God created Adam and Eve and told them that they should not go to the Tree of Knowledge, and they should not eat the fruit of it — then He became the serpent! coiled around the tree, and seduced Eve to eat the fruit of the tree. God Himself became the serpent!

I love this story. Christians will be very much shocked. But only God can do such a thing — nobody else. From where can the serpent come? And without God's help, how can the serpent convince Eve? In fact, the whole thing was decided beforehand : God wanted man to go astray, because only by going astray does one become mature. God wanted man to commit sin, because only through sin does one one day arrive at sainthood. There is no other way.

That's why God said : "Don't eat the fruit of this tree!" This is simple psychology. What Christians say, if THEY are true, means that God is not even as much a psychologist as Freud is. This is simple psychology, that if you prevent somebody from something, that something becomes more attractive, more magnetic.

If you say, "DON'T do this!" you can be sure it will be done. Every parent knows this, and God is the ultimate parent. Will He not know it?

There is a story : Freud had gone in a garden with his wife and child, and they walked around and it was a beautiful spring evening. They forgot about the child, and then it was time for the closing; the bell was ringing and everybody was to get out. The wife was very much disturbed and she said, "But where is the child? He has disappeared!" And it was a big park.

Freud said, "Tell me only one thing : did you prevent him from going somewhere?"

And she said, "Yes, I told him not to go to the fountain."

Then he said, "Let us go. If my insight is right, he will be there at the fountain."

And he was found at the fountain.

The wife was very much puzzled; she said, "How could you know?"

Freud said, "This is simple psychology. Every parent should know."

No, I cannot trust the Christian interpretation, because that makes God look very foolish. I would like Him to do what I am saying! He must have planned it, knowing perfectly well that if Adam is prevented from eating, is told, commanded, ordered, if an absolute order is given, "NEVER touch the fruit of that tree!" then it is absolutely certain that he will eat it.

But maybe... Adam was the first man and was not aware of the ways of man yet, was the first child and may have been an obedient child. There are obedient people also. And God must have waited for a few days and Adam had not gone to the tree; He must have become the serpent. Now He must have tried through the woman, because when you cannot do anything to the man, the right way is through the woman. He must have tried through the woman. He must have talked to Eve. He succeeded.

That's why I say the serpent and the saviour are one.

And in the East, the serpent has never been in the service of the Devil; it has always been in the service of God. In the East, this is our symbology : that the serpent is inside you, coiled at your sex centre; it is called KUNDALINI — coiled serpent. It is THERE, asleep, at the lowest rung. The tree of life is your spine — that holds your life, it is your trunk. It nourishes you, your shape runs through it, and the serpent is lying there.

When anything stirs you it will stir the serpent too —because that is your energy. That is WHERE your energy is. So, Barkha, don't be worried, don't feel guilty. That's my essential message to you : Never feel guilty for anything! All that happens is good. THE BAD DOES NOT HAPPEN and cannot happen, because the world is SO full of God, how can the bad happen? The bad must be our interpretation.

So let me say to you : sex and samadhi are the same energy. The serpent and the saviour are not two. There is a link between the lowest and the highest. There is a sequence that leads from one to the other, a way of life, a way of love, natural and inevitable as the way of a growing tree.

Have you watched a tree growing, how it grows, how it goes on groping and growing? What method does it follow? From the seed, the sprout, and then slowly, slowly, it starts rising upwards. It comes from deep down in the earth, and then it starts rising into the sky. From root to trunk and branch and leaf and flower and fruit.... This is my message for your tree of life too.

There is no distinction between the sacred and the profane, no separation between God who is love and the human-animal four-lettered love. It is one continuity. Your love and God's love are two ends of the same phenomenon, of the same energy.

Your love is too muddy, true; too full of many other things — hatred, anger, jealousy, possessiveness — true. But still it is gold — mixed with mud, but still it is gold. You have to pass through fire, and all that is not gold will be gone and only gold will remain.

And I am the fire! the Master is the fire. Pass through me — unafraid, unashamed. Pass through me fearlessly. I accept you as you are : you also accept yourself, because only through acceptance is the transformation possible, otherwise not. If you start feeling guilty, you will become repressive.

Have you gone to Khajuraho or Konarak? There you will see

what I am saying to you. Those are Tantra temples, the MOST sacred temples that still exist on the earth; all other temples are ordinary, bourgeois. Only Khajuraho and Konarak, these two temples, have a different message which is not ordinary, which is extraordinary. Extraordinary because it is true.

What is their message?

If you have been to these temples, you will be surprised that on the outer sunlit walls there are ALL kinds of sexual postures — men and women making love in so many postures! conceivable and inconceivable, possible and impossible. All the walls are full of sex. One is shocked. One starts feeling : What obscenity! One wants to condemn, one wants to lower one's eyes. One wants to escape. But that is not because of the temple but because of the priest AND his poison inside you.

Go inside. As you start moving inside the temple, the figures are less and less, and love starts changing. On the outer walls it is pure sexuality; as you start entering inside, you will find sex is disappearing. Couples are still there, in deep love, looking into each other's eyes, holding hands, embracing each other, but sexuality is no more there. Go still deeper — figures are even less. Couples are still there, but not even holding hands, not even touching. Go still deeper — and the couples have disappeared. Go still deeper....

At the innermost core of the temple what in the East we call the GHARBA, the womb — there is not a single figure. The crowd is gone, the many is gone. There is not even a window for the outside! No light comes from the outside; it is utter darkness, silence, calm and quiet. And there is not even a figure of a god — it is emptiness, it is nothingness.

The innermost core is nothingness and the outermost core is a carnival. The innermost core is meditation, samadhi, and the outermost core is sexuality. This is the whole life of man depicted.

But remember : if you destroy the outer walls, you will destroy the inner shrine too — because the innermost silence and darkness cannot exist without the outer walls. The centre of the cyclone cannot exist without the cyclone. The centre cannot exist without the circumference. They are together!

Your outermost life is full of sexuality — perfectly good and perfectly beautiful! Khajuraho simply depicts you. It is the human story in stone; it is the human dance in stone —from the lowest to the highest rung, from the many to one, from love to meditation, from the other to one's own emptiness and aloneness.

Courageous were the people who created these temples. And they had a vision that is my approach too. Tantra is my approach. The still point is shown together with the turning world.

The way of Tantra is not one of blind sensuality — and not only of spirituality either. It is of both/and. Tantra does not believe in the philosophy of either/or : it believes in the philosophy of both/and. It does not reject anything — it transforms everything. Only cowards reject. And if you reject something you will be that much poorer — because something has been left untransformed. A part of you will remain ungrown; a part of you will remain childish. Your maturity will never be total. It will be like your one leg remains on the first rung and your hand has reached to the last rung : you will be stretched along this polarity and you will be in anguish, in agony; your life will not be of ecstasy.

That's why I say I preach Epicurus and Buddha together to you. Epicurus remains with the outer wall of the Khajuraho temple; he is right as far as he goes, but he does not go far enough. He simply takes a walk around the temple and goes home; he is not aware that he has missed the very point of the temple. Those outer walls are only outer walls; they exist for the inner shrine.

Buddha goes into the inner shrine, sits there. In that silence he remains, but he forgets about the outer wall. And without the outer wall there is no inner shrine.

To me, both are lopsided, half-half. Something has been rejected and something has been chosen — they have not been choiceless. I say to you : Accept all! the outer and the inner, the without and the within, and you will be the richest sannyasins upon the earth.

Drop guilt!

Tantra is the whole way — neither obsession with the world, nor withdrawal from it. It is being in the world lightly, with a little smile. It is playfulness. It doesn't take things seriously. It is light of heart, it laughs. It is unashamedly earthly and infinitely other-earthly. The earth and the sky meet in Tantra; it is the meeting of polar opposites.

SO, BARKHA, YOU NEED NOT BE WORRIED about a sudden stirring of your sexual energy. It is how it should be!

You say: TODAY AFTER LECTURE, AS I WAS KNEELING BEFORE YOUR PLATFORM, SEXUAL FANTASIES CONCERNING YOU FILLED MY HEAD. ON THE ONE HAND, MY BODY WAS FILLED WITH ENERGY AND IT FELT GOOD...

Listen to the body. The body is wiser than your so-called mind. The body knows much more, and the body is ninety-nine percent of your energy; mind is a small fragment — making too much fuss.

ON THE OTHER HAND, I BEGAN TO FEEL GUILTY...

The priest came in; the Christian started speaking, the church. You have to be aware. You are not to allow the church to go on victimizing you forever. You have to drop the church, not your sexuality! because the sexuality will become the outer wall of your temple, and the church will never allow you growth.

AND ON THE OTHER HAND I BEGAN TO FEEL GUILTY, THAT IT WAS WRONG TO HAVE SUCH THOUGHTS ABOUT YOU AND I SHOULDN'T ALLOW THEM TO CONTINUE. THEN MY STOMACH BEGAN CRAMPING AND I HAD TO RUN TO THE BATHROOM WITH DIARRHOEA. WHAT IS HAPPENING? AND IS IT OKAY TO HAVE SUCH FANTASIES?

The diarrhoea came because you crushed your rising energy, you repressed. The priest poisoned your stomach. Now, if you go to the priest he will say it is because of your sexuality that you got disturbed. He will use it again to give you new guilt.

He will say, "Look : it is your sexuality that has disturbed you."
It is NOT your sexuality that has disturbed you : it is your idea
of guilt that has disturbed you. Sexuality was innocent and pure.
The idea of guilt is impure, calculating, cunning.

Drop such ideas! Listen to the body and go with the body.
And soon you will see... sexuality is changing into spirituality.

I have heard :

The sculptor, Bernini, made the moment of orgasm his model
for St. Teresa's experience of union with God.

He searched for a model. He wanted to make a statue of
St. Teresa in the state of samadhi. He searched for the model —
he could not find... except a woman in orgasm.

I love the story. Yes, that is true — I agree with Bernini
absolutely. You cannot find anything else which can depict
ecstasy, which can symbolize ecstasy. For the moment, a woman
in orgasm IS in samadhi — although for the moment only. Soon
the moment will be gone and she will plunge into deep darkness.

And the woman's orgasm is deeper than the man's, because
the man's orgasm has become very local. It is confined to his
genitalia; his whole body remains unaffected. But if a woman
goes into orgasm, if she goes, then her whole body goes into
it. She is more total, more rounded, more of a whole. And when
her whole body is throbbing with joy, is moving in a timeless
moment, is no more part of a thinking process, all thoughts have
disappeared, and there is great silence — yes, only that can
depict....

And that has been the insight of all the saints who have
attained. Whenever they have talked about God and the experience
of God's meeting, they have always brought the metaphor from sex.
It has to be orgasm — it is the ULTIMATE orgasm, it is the TOTAL
orgasm, it is the ETERNAL orgasm. But where can you find the right
expression for it? You can find it only in the moment, the
momentary orgasm, that sex makes possible for humanity to attain.

If you go to Khajuraho, you will see that : on every lover's
face that is sculpted on the outer walls, great ecstasy. So

many people go to Khajuraho and Konarak, but they only look at the lower half of these figures; they become concentrated on the genitalia. Very few people have been able to see the whole figures. And, certainly, rarely has somebody been able to see the faces of the figures — because you are so much obsessed with sexuality, for or against, that you remain confined to the lower.

If you go and see Khajuraho, don't miss the FACES of the lovers — they have the real message. Those faces are so blissful, so calm, so meditative, that you will not find such faces sculpted anywhere else. Such great ecstasy! Even the stone has bloomed in those faces; those faces have transformed the stone into roseflowers, into lotuses. Seeing those faces you will be able to see that these lovers are no more part of time and space; they have gone beyond.

The figures are sexually active, but they are not obsessed with sex — neither for nor against. Both are obsessions — for and against simply means things are no longer natural. When things are natural, you are neither for nor against.

Are you for sleep or against sleep? If you are for, you have become unnatural; if you are against, you have become unnatural. One is not for or against sleep! It is just a natural thing — so is sex. And when sex is accepted naturally, it starts growing higher. Then one day, the bud spontaneously becomes a flower. Not that you have to DO something — just let the energy move! let the sap flow and the bud WILL become the flower.

Those faces are utterly at ease, in a state of let-go. They are in the world, but not of it. And they are not doing anything; they are just like small children playing on the sea beach. They are playful. But sexually obsessed people have been very much against Khajuraho. Mahatma Gandhi wanted it to be covered with mud so that only once in a while, when some special guest came from the West or from the East it could be uncovered for him. It should be closed for ordinary people.

Mahatma Gandhi represents the mediocre mind — he is the mahatma of the mediocres. He represents the sexual obsession.

His whole life he was obsessed against sex. Now, if Mahatma Gandhi goes to see Khajuraho, I don't think he will be able to see the faces of the figures; I don't think he will be able to go inside the temple — the outer will be enough to prevent him. And I don't think he will be able to watch even the outer; he will be so angry, he will feel so guilty, he will feel so ashamed! If you talk to the so-called educated Indians about Khajuraho, you will see they feel ashamed. They will say to you, "We are sorry, but these temples don't represent our mainstream. They are not representative of our culture. They are AGAINST our culture. They are freak events in our culture — they don't represent us. We are very sorry that they exist."

But they represent one of the most wholistic attitudes towards life — all is accepted, because all is divine.

So, Barkha, allow your sexual energies to move. Go with them. Don't fight with them; they are your energies. Float with them and they will take you to the ocean. They INEVITABLY take you! You just have to be capable of letting go.

To me, the final stage of a human being is not the sage, not the Buddha, but Shiva Nataraj — Shiva the Dancer. Buddha has gone very deep, but the outer wall is missing, the outer wall is denied. Shiva contains all, contains all contradictions — contains the whole of God choicelessly. He lives in the innermost core of the shrine and dances on the outer walls too.

Unless the sage can dance, something is missing.

Life is a dance. You have to participate in it. And the more silent you become, the deeper your participation. Never withdraw from life. Never renounce life, because in renouncing life you will be renouncing God Himself. Be true to life, be committed to life. Be utterly for life.

It happens when you have reached to the innermost core of the temple... there is no reason for you to dance; you can remain there silent. Just as Buddha says : When you have attained enlightenment, then there are two paths open for you — either you can become an ARHAT, you can go to the other shore, or you can become a BODHISATTVA, you can remain on this shore.

In fact, there is no reason to be on this shore when you have become enlightened. But Buddha says for the sake of others, for compassion's sake, create great compassion in yourself so that you can linger a little longer and help people.

In the same way I would like to say to you : When you become enlightened, two possibilities open — either you can remain inside the temple, in the womb of the temple... dark, windowless, not going out at all, not even a light penetrates; no sound from the outside, nothing of the marketplace. You sit silently there, in absolute silence, in timeless silence. There is NO reason why you should come out and have a dance, but still I would like you to come back, although there is no reason. You can stop there; your journey is complete — but something is still missing. You have learnt how to be silent, now you have to show whether you can be silent in sound. You have learnt how to be alone, now you have to show whether you can be alone and love too. You have to come back to the marketplace from the mountains. The ultimate test is there.

There is NO reason for this, that I would like to repeat. There is no reason for this world, but there is a rhyme and a rhythm — no reason, but a rhyme and a rhythm. When you have become silent, create sound — and your silence will go deeper because of the contrasting sound. When you have known what aloneness is, be together with people —and the people and their presence will help you to know your aloneness far more deeply. When you have known how to remain still, dance — and the dance will give you the background in which the stillness will come very loud and very clear.

There is no reason for it, but there is a rhyme and a rhythm in it. Go to the opposite! And that is the meaning of Shiva Nataraj — Shiva the Dancer of dancers. It is hard, he is a Buddha, but in his outer activities he is a worldly man.

This is the ultimate for Tantra, and this is the ultimate for me too. I would like you to become gods and yet part of this world. No withdrawal is needed. But if you have a guilt feeling somewhere, the moment you become silent you will not be able to come back to the world of sound and noise. Drop all guilt feelings. That will help you to grow to the ultimate, and that will help you to come back to the world too.

When you can come back to the marketplace with a wine bottle in your hand, the ultimate is achieved.

The fourth question :

What is philosophy?

A small anecdote :

A SPORTING GENTLEMAN at a bar insisted that blindfolded, he could taste any liquor and identify it, and tell the name of the company that produced it.

The bartender accepted the challenge. After the gentleman was blindfolded, the barflies gathered round to witness the first test. The expert took a sip, and immediately declared : "Four Roses, put out by Frankfort Distillers."

"Right," replied the bartender. They would try again. On his next turn, the expert again took only the one sip and announced, "Canadian Club, put out by Hiram Walker."

"Right again," said the bartender. "Let's try just once more."

This time the gang thought they'd play a trick on him. Instead of whiskey, the bartender filled the bottle with urine.

. When the expert tasted this, he remarked excitedly, "Why, this is piss!"

"Right you are!" acknowledged the bartender. "But whose?"

Philosophy is unnecessary curiosity. Pointless curiosity. And you can go on and on... ad nauseam. Avoid! Philosophy has trapped many people and destroyed their lives.

Philosophy is mind gymnastics, hair-splitting. One can become very much, deeply involved in it. It is very very engrossing, because one question leads to ten new questions and so on and so forth.... But you are in a mind trip; it leads you away and away from life and life's real problems. It leads you away from existence. You become obsessed with speculation and you forget living.

That's why I say art is far better, because it is far more earthly. Philosophy is abstract. Avoid abstractions, because through abstraction you will never come to reality. And we HAVE to come to reality — because you can only eat real bread, not a philosophic concept of bread. You can love only a real woman, not a philosophic abstraction of womanhood. When you want to drink water and you are thirsty, you would not like any philosophy about water; you would like real water — howsoever muddy and dirty, but real water. Even Pune water will do! But you would not like philosophy about water.

Philosophy is always about and about; it goes round and round in circles — it never arrives anywhere.

The fifth question :

Your words about priests ring so true to me and are body blows to my ego. Yet my mind goes on asking : was the celibate monk, Francis of Assisi, not enlightened?

SAMUDRA, FRANCIS OF ASSISI WAS ENLIGHTENED — not because he was a monk, but in spite of it. It is like a man taking part in a race carrying two rocks in his two hands and he arrives first — not because of those two rocks that he has been carrying in his hands, but in spite of them. It is a miracle that St. Francis ever became enlightened.

You need not carry those rocks.

He must have been a rare man — that even remaining a Christian he became enlightened.

The sixth question :

I want to become a sannyasin, but I am very serious about it. And I have been thinking and thinking, but no conclusion seems to be in sight.

TO TAKE SANNYAS SERIOUSLY IS TO MISS THE WHOLE point

of it. Sannyas is laughter, playfulness, fun. Laughter is at the very heart of it. You can only take it playfully, not seriously.

If you decide out of long long thinking about it, your decision will be wrong. If you come to a conclusion I will not suggest to you that you take sannyas. You have started from a wrong beginning. The whole point of sannyas is to take life non-seriously, playfully, lightly. And if you can take life lightly, you will be able to walk without feet, fly without wings, think without mind.

I have heard that angels in heaven can fly, not because they have wings, but because they take themselves very lightly.

Bonhoeffer, a Christian mystic who was murdered by Adolf Hitler, wrote from prison his last letter to his friends. In that letter I have come across a great message. He says : "Make the most of the beautiful country you are in. Spread HILARITAS around you — and mind you keep it yourself too!"

Hilaritas — hilarity — this country is beautiful! This moment, this space is beautiful, where you find yourself. Nothing is missing except your laughter. If you can laugh, you will fall in tune with the cosmic energy. I teach you laughter. I am against all seriousness.

Either take sannyas or don't take it — but don't think about it, because that is a sure way to miss it. You can take it after thinking but you will miss it all the same.

Sannyas is a state of living unison, of being who we are and where, with widest eyes. Paradise is regained in the recognition that it was never lost. We waken from the long dream of having left it, and find ourselves at home all the while.

You have not gone anywhere, you have not left the home. You have NOT fallen! You are ALREADY in the Garden of Eden, just fallen asleep. Sannyas is an awakening. And if you can laugh, you will awaken and you will awaken others too.

I teach you a life of joy, celebration, delight. I don't teach you long faces. The days of the sad saint are no more. The future belongs to the laughing saints.

And the last question :

There is no doubt that for ninety-nine percent of the lectures I am very busy thinking. But strange are the

weird trips I get into! Now for the last ten days, I am
most of the time involved in these ballerina fantasies —
seeing myself in this beautiful tutu, whirling in front
of you in a great symphony!

The dream of a poor little elephant?

RADHA, THAT IS GREAT! Forget all about the lectures! You are
having such a beautiful experience — even I felt jealous.

And the really really last one:

I have known many many successes and only a few
failures in my life, but still those few failures are heavy
on me, they hurt. Why?

BE A LITTLE PLAYFUL, MAN. If you go on succeeding in
everything, then everybody else will go on failing. A few chances
to others too — be a little fair.

A story for you to meditate...

Joe the gambler walked into a saloon and said to the
bartender, "Bet you a dollar I can bite my right eye."

The bartender said, "Okay. It's a bet."

So Joe took out his glass eye and bit it. The bartender paid
up, and then challenged, "Bet you a dollar you can't bite your
left eye."

Joe accepted the challenge. A crowd gathered. He then
removed his dental plates from his mouth and bit his left eye.
The bartender smiled and paid up.

Then Joe said, "I'll bet you a dollar I can piss on you without
getting you wet."

This offer was promptly accepted, and then Joe proceeded
to do his thing. The bartender jumped back, drenched, and
exclaimed, "What? What the hell are you doing?"

"Well," answered Joe ruefully, as he slapped a buck on the
bar, "You can't win 'em all!"

Notes

Notes

Notes

Notes